This work is dedicated to Mary McFarland,
my best friend for the past thirty-four years.

Contents

Materials Found on Accompanying CD-ROM*

Facilitator's Guide to Real-Time Strategic Planning *(materials you can use to conduct a one-day Real-Time Strategic Planning kick-off session)*

This material can also be downloaded from http://www.FieldstoneAlliance.org/worksheets. Simply enter this URL in your web browser and use the code W657Nsr08 to download the tools.

Tools

Essential Tools for Forming Strategy (electronic versions of the tools found in Part Two)

Tool 1: Current Business Model

Tool 2: Financial Analysis

Tool 3: Competitor Analysis

Tool 4: Trend Analysis

Tool 5: Future Business Model

Tool 6: Identity Statement

Tool 7: Strategy Screen

Tool 8: Big Question

Tool 9: Next Steps Work Plan

Tool 10: Strategy Road Map

Supplemental Tools

Tool 11: Market Position and Strategy Analysis

Tool 12: Community Meeting

Tool 13: Identify and Establish a Nonprofit Brand

Tool 14: Strategic Thinkers Group

Tool 15: Expert Interviews

Tool 16: Reading Group

Tool 17: Brainstorming Process

Tool 18: Scenario Thinking

Tool 19: Value Creation Cycle

Tool 20: Mission Statement Refinement

Tool 21: Organizational Self-Assessment and Discussion

Tool 22: The Due Diligence Tool

Tool 23: Opportunity Matrix

Tool 24: Logic Model

Tool 25: 90-Day Plan for Incremental Improvements

Tool 26: Post-Action Debriefing

Tool 27: Traditional Strategic Plan Template

Nonprofit Strategy Revolutionary Certificate

*NOTE: The CD-ROM has been replaced with a link to download the files online; all materials from the CD-ROM can be accessed using the URL and code found on page 183.

Acknowledgments

A PROJECT OF THIS SCOPE would not have been possible without the support of a group of dedicated and forward-looking funders. I am grateful to the project's supporters, including Tom Reis of the W.K. Kellogg Foundation, Kelvin Taketa and Chris Van Bergeijk of the Hawai'i Community Foundation, Stephanie McAuliffe of the David and Lucile Packard Foundation, Linda Wood of the Evelyn and Walter Haas, Jr. Fund, Mike Bailin (formerly) and Jamie McAuliffe of the Edna McConnell Clark Foundation, Janet Sarbaugh of the Heinz Endowments, Gregg Behr (formerly) of The Forbes Funds, Scott Izzo of the Richard King Mellon Foundation, and Rick Moyers of the Meyer Foundation. They provided both material support and, through our funders' advisory group, intellectual sustenance and practical feedback along our four-year journey.

Every research and development project at La Piana Associates is a team effort involving many of our talented staff members. This one was no exception. We regularly devote time at staff meetings and our regular multi-day retreats to testing out new ideas. There is also a synergy that comes from our shared work on client engagements. So, in a very real sense, the entire staff is part of our development process. The four-year project leading to the creation of the approach we call *Real-Time Strategic Planning* was managed by Michaela Hayes, a seasoned researcher. Other management and consulting staff who were intimately involved in the project, including the multiple pilot efforts, were Bill Coy, Liza Culick, Jo DeBolt, Robert Harrington, Lester Olmstead-Rose, and Vance Yoshida. Kristen Godard, Shiree Teng, and Melissa Mendes Campos helped bring some of the tools to life. Mary Stelletello, who joined the firm as the first draft was nearing completion, brought a fresh pair of eyes to the entire work, revamped the tools, and made essential contributions to the quality of the final product. Jim Thomas, our independent evaluator, provided extremely helpful feedback while the project was underway, not just a report card at the end. In fact, he became a true learning partner with us.

I worked closely on this book with Michaela Hayes, with whom I also collaborated on an earlier project, *Play to Win: The Nonprofit Guide to Competitive Strategy*.[1] Her advice and help were irreplaceable, but the conclusions and recommendations contained herein, for better or worse, are my own.

It is fitting that this book is published by Fieldstone Alliance (formerly Amherst H. Wilder Foundation Publishing). Bryan Barry's *Strategic Planning Workbook*, first published in1987, in a real sense kicked off the strategic planning boom in the sector.[2] Now, some twenty years later, Fieldstone Alliance, and my longtime editor Vince Hyman, are returning to the topic with an entirely new—even revolutionary—approach. Thank you, Bryan, for inspiring my interest in strategy as a young executive director.

I am also indebted to the legions of consultants who paved the way for this book by experimenting with more creative approaches to strategy. In particular, I want to acknowledge the work of Mike Allison and Jude Kaye, longtime colleagues and coauthors of *Strategic Planning for Nonprofit Organizations*,[3] and also the work of John Bryson, whom I have studied from as far back as graduate school (in particular, his seminal book *Strategic Planning for Public and Nonprofit Organizations*).[4] This book builds on their work and that of countless others.

---

[1]   David La Piana with Michaela Hayes, *Play to Win: The Nonprofit Guide to Competitive Strategy* (San Francisco: Jossey-Bass, 2005).

[2]   Bryan W. Barry, *Strategic Planning Workbook for Nonprofit Organizations* (Saint Paul, MN: Fieldstone Alliance, 1987).

[3]   Mike Allison and Jude Kaye, *Strategic Planning for Nonprofit Organizations,* 2nd ed. (San Francisco: Jossey-Bass, 2005).

[4]   John Bryson, *Strategic Planning for Public and Nonprofit Organizations: A Guide to Strengthening and Sustaining Organizational Achievement* (San Francisco: Jossey-Bass, 1995).

Preface:
Welcome to the Revolution

If I can't dance, I don't want to be part of your revolution.
—Emma Goldman[5]

WELCOME! By opening this book you have already told me three important things about yourself. First, that you care deeply about a nonprofit organization, or perhaps about a whole array of nonprofits, you are or have been involved with. Second, that you are either in a leadership position in a nonprofit, a foundation, or a consultancy serving nonprofits; or you plan to be such a leader in the future. And third, (I can guess) that you are frustrated and dissatisfied with the traditional approach to strategic planning that you may have experienced.

Then again, if you are contemplating a strategic planning process, maybe you picked up this book because you want to ensure that your organization's investment of time and money yields something of commensurate value. Perhaps you are uncertain whether the traditional strategic planning approach—the type you've read about, experienced, and had recommended by consultants—will do the trick.

These concerns are widespread. La Piana Associates has worked with hundreds of nonprofit and foundation leaders who share your frustrations. In the course of research during the development of this book, I heard consistent complaints about the time, money, and effort that go into traditional strategic planning, and the often-puny yield in terms of genuinely useful strategic direction and progress. As a result, I had to pause and ask, *why do*

---

[5] As quoted at http://en.wikiquote.org/wiki/Emma_Goldman.

we keep doing it this way? You may have heard the adage that the definition of insanity is to do the same thing repeatedly while expecting a different result. Traditional nonprofit strategic planning may not be insane, but it is certainly inefficient, lacking in power, and as of now, outmoded. It is high time for a revolution in our approach to strategic thinking in the sector. And, staying true to Emma Goldman's hedonistic spirit, this new approach should also be a lot more fun than traditional strategic planning.

In this book, I explore alternative ways of forming *strategies*—patterns of behavior that can help your organization achieve its mission. The ideas and tools I present go beyond traditional nonprofit strategic planning methods, and our research suggests they can be more effective. Along the way, I offer a new context for some familiar and traditional strategic planning activities, such as the environmental scan.

Make no mistake, these activities can be useful. I do not intend to throw the strategic baby out with the planning bath water. Instead, I want to help you take the best of traditional strategic planning, recontextualize it in a more flexible and powerful way, and augment it with tools that can fuel ongoing strategic thinking and acting throughout your organization. I invite you to become the spark of a grassroots strategy uprising. Together we can fan that spark into the fire of a nonprofit strategy revolution.

Nonprofits stick with traditional approaches to strategic planning despite their widespread dissatisfaction for one principal reason: they have no alternatives to choose from. In fact, the only term in general use to discuss "strategy" in the sector is "strategic planning," as if the *process* (in this case planning) and its *object* (forming strategy) were one and the same. The new books and articles on strategic planning that regularly appear offer variations on the traditional theme. They alter the steps in the process, their order, or their relative emphasis, and they may bring new technologies to bear. Meanwhile, through our team's research on the ground with real nonprofit organizations, we have come to believe that it is not the process, the quality of the work done, or the precise order of the steps that make traditional strategic planning such a frustrating tool. The problem is more basic than that. The evidence that traditional strategic planning improves an organization's performance is, at best, very mixed.

We think nonprofits can do better. Consider these nuggets from *Business Performance Measurement* by Andy Neely:[6]

> This failure of strategic planning to create focus and achieve results is reflected in the findings from executives we have surveyed. . . . Typically between 60 and 80 percent of respondents to these surveys express strong dissatisfaction with the strategic planning processes in their organizations. The principal reasons cited for these concerns include plans that lack focus, failure to implement strategy effectively, and failure to follow up and to demand accountability. (156–57)

> The failure of many strategic planning processes, and by extension the lack of organizational performance, is a result of the inability of the process, as implemented, to create focus among those executives charged with developing strategy, on the few challenges and opportunities that are critical to the future viability and success of the organization. (158–59)

> In too many strategic planning activities, there is not enough mental toughness, political will, or shared understanding achieved to reduce the strategic agenda to a realistic and manageable *critical few* . . . it is difficult for strategists to identify the same array of options for the firm, and even more difficult for them to agree on implementation approaches. Unless the right process is employed, strategic planning becomes a *list*-making activity—long lists of opportunities, capabilities, and things to do, with no real sense of priority. (172)

And this one from Keith McFarland's "A Better Scheme for Strategic Planning": "Today, traditional strategic planning may sometimes cost companies more than it contributes. More importantly, they often get in the way of real work—especially in small to midsize businesses, where quick adaptation is the key to survival."[7]

The focus of traditional strategic planning is to produce a formal written document, within a preset time frame, that will "endure" for a predetermined length of time (usually three years), and cover a predetermined list

---

[6] Andy Neely, ed., *Business Performance Measurement* (Cambridge: Cambridge University Press, 2002).

[7] Keith McFarland, "A Better Scheme for Strategic Planning," BusinessWeek.com (January 19, 2005), www.businessweek.com/smallbiz/content/jan2005/sb20050119_9832_sb037.htm.

of areas with very specific (and often distant) goals and objectives. This focus is just not compatible with the formation of effective strategy in a functioning nonprofit in today's rapid-response world. Or, as McGill University business professor Henry Mintzberg put it to me much more succinctly: "Strategy is not planning." He explained that the structures and processes characteristic of planning often stymie the necessary fluidity and organic nature of real strategy formation.[8]

I suspect that you understand implicitly what I mean by a rapid-response world. It is your daily experience. When I started out in nonprofits, someone would have a question, handwrite a letter, have it typed, then make corrections, and have a final version retyped. Finally the letter would be put in an envelope and mailed to me. I would receive the letter a couple of days later, read it, consider my reaction, handwrite a response, and so on. The process from the point of someone posing a question for me to receiving my response could take a week or more. Nowadays, of course, e-mail shrinks that week to a few moments.

The rapid-response world is not just the result of advances in individual communications technology. Technology has sped up organizational decision-making and facilitated the fast-changing environment in which we work. In a rapid-response world you cannot make a strategic decision and expect it to meet your organization's needs for years (sometimes even for months). Today you need faster—indeed continuous—processes for responding to your environment.

And that is the flaw in the current state of the art: traditional strategic plans, once complete, are not fluid and organic but static—and they quickly grow stale. Since variations on the traditional strategic planning theme all share this same basic flaw, it is not surprising that none of them can reliably and efficiently produce the result nonprofit leaders are looking for when they decide to undertake strategic planning: more powerful strategies that will enhance their organization's success.

Clearly, nonprofits need a new paradigm of strategy formation. The rapid-response world in which we live requires nonprofits to identify, understand, and act upon new information and dynamically changing situations in real time; that means now, not in six months. But making the shift to a new and faster approach to strategy will not be easy. Funders are accustomed to seeing a traditional strategic planning document from prospective grantees; consultants (including La Piana Associates) have built successful strategic

---

[8]   E-mail communication from Henry Mintzberg to David La Piana, 5 May 2007.

planning practices; and the available written resources on the subject emphasize the importance, indeed the indispensability, of strategic planning. It will require more than another new approach, different terminology, or a nifty set of variations to loosen the grasp of traditional strategic planning on the sector; it will take a nonprofit strategy revolution—an altogether different way of thinking about strategy. The words *strategy* and *planning*, unlike other famous pairs such as peanut butter and jelly, stars and stripes, or Laurel and Hardy, need not always travel together.

In fact, the revolution has already begun. Every nonprofit leader who breaks out of the three-year planning cycle to form strategies as opportunities and challenges arise is manning the strategy revolution barricades. Every funder that asks its grantees to describe their strategy to combat a social problem rather than to simply submit a traditional strategic plan is storming the planning Bastille. And every consultant who, based on years of experience and accumulated wisdom, innovates, blows up the process, or instinctively tries a nontraditional approach with a client, is a strategic planning maverick—true revolutionaries all. Welcome to the revolution.

The Seeds of Revolution: The Strategy Formation Project

This book is the product of a four-year research and development effort at La Piana Associates. The Strategy Formation Project (2003–2007) was initially conceived as an investigation into the limitations of traditional strategic planning. The pleas of the nonprofit leaders and funders we met ("You're going to find a better way, right?" and "Thank God you're doing this; strategic planning is *such* a waste of time!") convinced us early on that the project needed to evolve into a general effort to find alternatives that are more useful than the traditional ways in which nonprofits undertake strategic planning. The project grew in scope and intensity with the following elements:[9]

- A review of the enormous (mostly business) literature on strategic management (the larger field in which we find strategic planning)

- Interviews with two dozen nonprofit leaders

---

[9]   For a full description of project elements and a list of the pilot participants, interviewees, and other key informants, see The Strategy Formation Project, www.lapiana.org/consulting/research/sf.html.

- Interviews with "strategy gurus" whose opinions are widely respected
- Interviews with leading nonprofit capacity builders, colleagues in the larger work to increase the effectiveness and capacity of the nonprofit sector
- The creation of a methodology for piloting some of the new ideas our team developed or adapted
- Initial testing of these ideas with two groups of executive directors, totaling twenty nonprofit leaders, located in two states
- A series of one-day sessions with three organizations whose leaders we knew, and who were willing to be our first guinea pigs
- Six-month pilot efforts with thirty geographically (and otherwise) diverse nonprofits, staggered over a period of two years, resulting in the development of a new model, *Real-Time Strategic Planning*

The value and outcome of all this activity is for the reader to judge. However, I think it offers a significant step forward from the current state of the art. Hence the decision to write this book and share what we have learned. The learning has been, for the most part, quite practical. In fact, the mostly simple lessons our team internalized during the research process have transformed the way we undertake La Piana Associates' *own* strategy engagements with clients—clients who, in turn, consistently tell us that these new approaches and tools, Real-Time Strategic Planning, are powerful and eye-opening. We are living the revolution and seeing the benefits in more responsive and effective strategy formation and strategic thinking across a range of our clients. You will hear some of their voices in these pages.

A report on the Strategy Formation Project and an Independent Evaluator's Report supplement this book and are published on the Internet at both the publisher's web site and La Piana Associates' web site. The URLs for these reports are www.FieldstoneAlliance.org and www.lapiana.org/consulting/research/sf.html.

How to Use This Book

The Nonprofit Strategy Revolution is appropriate for both grassroots and larger nonprofits, those new to a formal consideration of strategy, and those with substantial strategic planning experience who seek alternative approaches. Our team began by selecting grassroots organizations as our pilots, understanding that they had the fewest resources to invest in traditional strategic planning processes and thus perhaps had the most to gain from a different, more flexible approach. However, we quickly began incorporating some of the thinking that emerged from our work with these grassroots groups into our general client work, which is often with much larger nonprofits. It turned out that the same approaches worked quite well with a diverse array of organizations of differing sizes and types, and that, in fact, grassroots groups were often more challenged than larger nonprofits to incorporate these approaches into their daily work.

You can read this book as an introduction to the concept of strategy among nonprofits, or you can use our Real-Time Strategic Planning model to create strategy for your own nonprofit. You can work through it chapter by chapter, since the material builds sequentially from one concept to the next, or you can go straight to the Facilitator's Guide on the enclosed CD to organize a strategy formation session, or to the other CD materials to explore and try out one or more of the tools presented there. The goal is to help you become a more powerful strategic thinker, not to require you to follow a specific process (*that* would be the traditional strategic planning approach). Use this book in whatever way suits your needs today, then come back to it tomorrow as new needs emerge. *(NOTE: CD material accessed by URL, p. 183)*

How this book is structured

This book is organized into three parts. Part 1 consists of nine chapters that make the case for a strategy revolution, explain the terms we use, and teach you how to take that revolution into your organization or consultancy. Part 2 consists of ten essential tools that are immediately necessary as you conduct a one-day strategy formation session, which usually kicks off a Real-Time Strategic Planning process. The third part, a facilitator's guide for conducting the one-day kick-off session, is included on the CD accompanying the book. You can print out and copy this material for your staff.[10] The CD also includes the ten essential tools for forming strategy from Part 2, plus numerous supplemental tools to help in strategy development and implementation. It includes all blank worksheets and handouts so you can print these as needed. As already noted, additional

---

[10] Note that because the kick-off session requires most of the ten essential tools, portions of those tools are duplicated in the Facilitator's Guide and relabeled as handouts and worksheets for use during the session. Rather than referring you to Part 2 to make copies, we felt it would make your life easier to repeat the information.

resources are available on the web at www.FieldstoneAlliance.org and www.lapiana.org/consulting/research/sf.html.

Following is a description of the sections of the book and supplements.

Part One: The Strategy Revolution

Chapter 1: Why a Strategy Revolution? presents nonprofit strategy in a new context, distinguishes strategy from strategic planning, reviews the failings of traditional strategic planning, and makes the case for a revolution in our approaches to strategy formation. Topics covered include

- What is strategy, and why do nonprofits need it?
- Strategy and strategic planning in nonprofits
- Problems with traditional strategic planning

Chapter 2: The Strategy Pyramid introduces a tool that provides a context for understanding the different levels of strategic issues that face a non-profit organization. It also deals with the essential issue of implementing strategies. Topics include

- How to think about nonprofit strategy
- Organizational, programmatic, and operational strategies
- Implementing strategies

Chapter 3: Understanding Organizational Strategy defines organizational strategy, the topmost section of the Strategy Pyramid. Topics include

- Mission and strategy
- What is organizational strategy?
- What does organizational strategy look like?
- Real-Time Strategic Planning

Chapter 4: Organizational Identity and Strategy Formation introduces the key concepts of business model, market awareness, and competitive advantage, and discusses when to consider forming a new strategy. Topics include

- Understanding organizational strategy essentials: business model, market awareness, and competitive advantage
- How strategy is formed from these elements

Chapter 5: Developing a Strategy Screen describes a tool that can be used to create organizational strategies that will drive a nonprofit's work for years to come. Topics include

- Introducing Strategy Screens
- The Opportunity Matrix
- Using Strategy Screens

Chapter 6: Big Questions, Strategy Formation, and Implementation introduces the concept of the strategic challenge and the Big Question, and describes how to address strategic questions. Topics include

- Understanding and facing Big Questions
- Identifying a Big Question
- Developing a strategy that fits the screen

Chapter 7: Forming Programmatic Strategies provides a framework for a nonprofit to consider the best programmatic path (the middle of the Strategy Pyramid) to advance its mission, or to review the effectiveness of its current programmatic strategies. Topics include

- What is programmatic strategy?
- Constructing a programmatic logic model
- Programmatic strategy in action (cases)
- Programmatic strategy essentials: Choosing what programs to offer, where to offer them, to whom, via what approaches, and within what limits and mandates
- When to form new programmatic strategies

Chapter 8: Forming Operational Strategies will be most helpful to organizations in which operational challenges (the base of the Strategy Pyramid) are formidable. Topics include

- What is operational strategy?
- Operational strategy in action (cases)
- Operational strategy essentials: What systems, policies, and processes do we need to be well-run and stable? What are our near-term human, financial, and facilities resource needs? What are our longer-term capital, staffing, and cash needs? What operational data do our leaders need for good decision making?
- When to form new operational strategies

Chapter 9: Putting It All Together synthesizes the book's lessons and awards the reader with a Nonprofit Strategy Revolutionary Certificate.

Part Two: Essential Tools for Forming Strategy

Based on our experience using Real-Time Strategic Planning with numerous organizations, the ten tools in this section are essential. They are:

- Tool 1: Current Business Model
- Tool 2: Financial Analysis
- Tool 3: Competitor Analysis
- Tool 4: Trend Analysis
- Tool 5: Future Business Model
- Tool 6: Identity Statement
- Tool 7: Strategy Screen
- Tool 8: Big Question
- Tool 9: Next Steps Work Plan
- Tool 10: Strategy Road Map

Part Three: Compact Disc

The enclosed CD includes the **Facilitator's Guide to Real-Time Strategic Planning.** This section contains everything you need to organize a Real-Time Strategic Planning kick-off session. The guide has been tested during our own strategy formation sessions. Included are the day's agenda, instructions for preparing flip charts, prework (in the form of worksheets) to be completed by the executive director, and handouts and worksheets to be provided during the course of the session. The session itself has an aggressive time line, but in our experience, organizations can successfully complete all the work in one day, provided they have prepared adequately and stick to the schedule.

Copies of all tools (both those for the strategy formation session and supplementary tools), handouts, and blank worksheets are also included on the CD accompanying this book. For fun, there's a Nonprofit Strategy Revolutionary Certificate for you as well.

References

This work is built on the previous efforts of many thoughtful people. The references in this section were all consulted during the development of this publication. In some cases, we interviewed authors of these works as well.

Index

The index covers material in the print portion of the text and includes the tools and other resources found on the CD. You can use a search function to find specific information on the CD.

Web Resources

Finally, you can read supplemental material on our strategy research at the following web sites.

The Strategy Formation Project provides background information on the four-year project that culminated in this book. It includes lists of people we interviewed, a description of the project's design, and other material of interest to readers who want to know more about the research behind this work. This is published at www.lapiana.org/consulting/research/sf.html.

An independent evaluator's report by Jim Thomas (who followed the project, reviewed and assessed our progress, and made innumerable suggestions for improvements to the project as it was taking place) is available at www.FieldstoneAlliance.org and www.lapiana.org/consulting/research/sf.html.

A note on replicating materials from this book and the CD

The materials in this book and on the enclosed CD are protected by international and domestic copyright laws and may not be reproduced or copied except as otherwise provided herein. The CD that accompanies the book *The Nonprofit Strategy Revolution: Real-Time Strategic Planning in a Rapid-Response World* may be loaded onto the computer of the person who purchased the book. You may reproduce the materials on this CD for use in your own organization's strategy formation processes. So long as the material is for use **within your organization**, by all means, use it widely. Please do not remove the copyright watermark from each page, as this is how the author and publisher protect the work.

These materials may not be used, reproduced, or duplicated for training other organizations in the Real-Time Strategic Planning process as expressed in this book. Rights to use the materials in this manner are available for a nominal fee from the Copyright Clearance Center at www.copyright.com.

Similarly, consultants who wish to use these materials may not purchase one copy of the book and then repeatedly copy or print out the materials for use with each new organization. The following options, both inexpensive, will suffice for such use.

- Contact the Copyright Clearance Center and purchase rights for reuse. This is important if you are going to be altering and adapting the worksheets; or

- Ask your client to purchase the book and to make the requisite copies from the CD.

If you do alter or adapt material from this book, you must send a copy to Fieldstone Alliance within sixty days of the creation of such materials. Further, such altered or adapted worksheet materials must maintain the copyright watermark and are considered works of the author. Finally, Fieldstone Alliance reserves the right to disallow use of altered or adapted materials solely within its discretion. *(NOTE: CD material accessed by URL, p. 183)*

Conclusion: **Creating Winning Strategies**

One caveat is important at this early point: the process outlined here starts with the assumption that you come to this book with a clear sense of and consensus regarding your organization's mission (the social good it intends to create). This book picks up at the point where your mission has been adopted. If you need help clarifying your mission, see my friend and colleague Emil Angelica's excellent book *The Fieldstone Alliance Nonprofit Guide to Crafting Effective Mission & Vision Statements.*[11] The CD enclosed with this

---

[11] Emil Angelica, *The Fieldstone Alliance Nonprofit Guide to Crafting Effective Mission & Vision Statements* (Saint Paul, MN: Fieldstone Alliance, 2001).

book includes a useful tool to help you with this step (see Tool 20: Mission Statement Refinement), but aside from that, this book does not directly treat the topic of mission statements. Similarly, every nonprofit needs effective systems for governance, management, and program delivery. Many excellent resources treat these challenges, but they too are outside the scope of this book. Our focus is on strategy.

Finally, remember that strategy formation is not a solo activity. It is an organizational undertaking—at its best, almost a communal effort. You should work with your board and staff colleagues: be sure to include anyone with an especially keen eye for new trends and issues that may impact your nonprofit, or for coming up with creative and effective strategies, or both. These may sound like the "usual suspects" for a strategic planning process—and they may be. But rather than asking them to participate in a tri-annual planning marathon resulting in a written document that most people will never look at again, you are instead inviting them to become partners in an ongoing struggle to understand the world in which they work and to devise strategies that will be effective in that changing landscape. During this process, you will learn and grow together. Still, you should broaden the circle beyond the usual participants so that the larger organization and its constituents, to the greatest extent possible, are brought into the discussion—through surveys, focus groups, electronic newsletter updates, and other means appropriate to your size and resources.

Additionally, as you consider your external environment (also known as your "market"), be sure to include in your discussions external stakeholders who have important perspectives and knowledge from which your organization can benefit. This group may include your customers, funders, donors, community leaders, experts in your field, policy leaders, and the media. You may want to consult Sections Two and Three of my previous book, *Play to Win: The Nonprofit Guide to Competitive Strategy,* for practical market research tools developed by my colleague Michaela Hayes.[12]

And now—prepare to join the revolution!

David La Piana
January 2008
Emeryville, California

---

[12] David La Piana with Michaela Hayes, *Play to Win: The Nonprofit Guide to Competitive Strategy* (San Francisco: Jossey-Bass, 2005), 63–184.

PART **ONE**

The Strategy Revolution

Chapter One:
Why a Strategy Revolution?

We have a "strategic plan." It's called doing things.

—Herb Kelleher, founder of Southwest Airlines[13]

THE YOUNG (just twenty-six years old) new executive director was hoping to find some guidance in the stack of dusty boxes he had just located in a dark corner of the storage room, behind the spare mop heads and disinfectant. After some deft detective work, he had learned that this was where he would locate the organization's strategic plan. He opened the top carton of the stack and slipped out an impressively bound thirty-page document. Clutching his find, he raced back to his office expectantly, closed the door, sat, and began to read. There was a brief preamble: the mission and vision, some nice words about a better future, a time when kids wouldn't need the kinds of mental health services his organization provided.

He skimmed that portion and turned the page. He found, with mounting excitement, that the next section contained lists of new staff positions to be created, equipment to be bought, and even a new building to be built. There was a ten-year phase-in of the new expenses. The organization desperately needed these additional staff, could put the new equipment to use, and certainly yearned for a bigger building. He read on, anxious for the plan, for the strategy, for the road map that would tell him how all these great things would be accomplished. At the end of the document he found a section labeled Financial Plan that, he quickly realized, simply itemized the costs of these new items, added them to the

---

[13] Herb Kelleher, as quoted by Tom Peters at www.slideshare.net/ddebowczyk/tom-peters-on-action.

existing operating budget, and thereby provided a ten-year fund-raising goal. That was it! There was no strategy for *how* to raise the money that would be needed, only the need itself. Disappointed beyond words, he realized this was a shopping list, not a "strategic plan," whatever that was. He recycled all of the remaining copies, four cartons' worth, thereby making room for more cleaning supplies in the cramped storage room.

—My first encounter with a nonprofit strategic plan, 1982

This book grew out of the widely reported dissatisfaction of nonprofit leaders, their funders, and even some consultants with the traditional tools and approaches available through "strategic planning." To fully grasp the need for a revolution in our approach to nonprofit strategy formation, you must first understand what strategy is, and then consider the ways in which the traditional approach to strategy comes up short. Herb Kelleher, founder of Southwest Airlines, reminds us that *action* is where the game is won or lost. Planning and action, while not mutually exclusive, are not exactly close companions, as the story above illustrates. In the course of this book, you will see that action should be much more closely aligned with strategy. Thoughtful, strategic action—based on data, intuition, experience, and good old trial and error—will trump planning every time.

What Is Strategy and Why Do Nonprofits Need It?

Strategy may be the most oft-spoken term in nonprofit and business life. Today it is common to hear everything from organizational planning to human resources management to philanthropy referred to as "strategic." What we really seem to be trying to convey in widely applying this modifier is that the activity being described is "important," "well thought out," or both. Certainly these are aspects of sound strategy: it had better be about something important to the organization, and if strategy is not well thought out it will likely bring more trouble than benefit. But these elements of good strategy fall short of the term's greater meaning.

Strategy has been defined differently by various management theorists. Early in our research, I read several definitions and put them together to form my favorite definition of strategy. Simply articulated, it is "an organized pattern of behavior toward an end." (For now, as we wade into the topic, we will use this as our working definition of strategy. In Chapter 3, I will introduce a more restrictive definition intended specifically for nonprofit organizations.)

Nonprofits, both explicitly and implicitly, create and use strategy to achieve a multitude of purposes. These range from the relatively straightforward, such as creating a system for financial record keeping and reporting ("our financial management strategy"), to more complex matters, such as achieving a desired market position ("our market strategy").

As suggested above, strategy is indeed important, and when well conceived, it is also well thought out. Above all, however, strategy is, or should be, an ever-evolving, ongoing attempt to determine the right approach—the best pattern of behavior—to achieve an organization's ends. As you shall see, well-formed organizational strategies are the best path for a nonprofit to advance its mission.

Sound strategy is at the heart of good nonprofit leadership. Over time, strategy (as distinct from strategic planning) accounts for much of the success a nonprofit experiences in advancing its mission, in part because good strategic decisions lead to improved financial and organizational sustainability. This is as true for the nation's largest nonprofits as it is for grassroots organizations where, due to limited working capital, the margin for strategic error may be quite small.

In the vignette at the beginning of this chapter I relate how, as a new executive director searching for a direction for my nonprofit, I was urged to consult the organization's strategic plan. Obviously, lots of work had gone into compiling this document, and, misguided though it was, not all of the effort was wasted. The organization knew what it needed. It just did not know how to get it. In other words, the "strategic" plan lacked strategy. This was because the board and management did not know what defined them as an organization, what set the organization apart from others, what competitors were in its market, and how it stacked up against them. What my organization really needed—and eventually developed—were strategies that could guide its actions. Strategy that would lead to new staffing (tenfold growth over the next ten years) and new buildings (we built one, remodeled a second, and acquired a third through a merger over the next seven years). Strategy, not a plan, built our success. Of course, we regularly undertook strategic planning, like all good nonprofits in the 1980s, but the results tended to be more helpful in guiding our annual operations than in setting our strategic direction.

Nonprofits must regularly determine and adjust their strategies on multiple levels. You already know this. You may ask yourself questions that are related to strategic concerns:

- What is our "business"?
- Who are our clients?
- What are our core competencies?
- Who are our competitors, and how do we stack up against them?
- What programs should we offer?
- How effective are we in achieving our annual goals and objectives?
- What is our position in the marketplace?
- What social, political, economic, and technological trends will impact us and how?
- How do we achieve long-term financial success?
- How do we measure success?

You may also ask more operationally oriented questions:

- How should we manage our limited (and precious) surplus cash?
- Do we have sufficient management capacity?
- Where can we find the best board members?
- Is our structure aligned with our policies, procedures, and goals?
- What sort of training program should we develop for our staff?
- What personnel policies do we need?
- Is our compensation competitive?
- How will we maintain our aging building?

These and similar questions must be articulated and answered, strategies must be formed to achieve the goals implicit in these answers, and those strategies must then be turned into actions the organization will take. Moreover, strategies must be reconsidered as often as key circumstances change—or the nonprofit risks losing touch with its community and market. When this happens, it will lose traction in its efforts to successfully pursue its mission and, as a result, it may become less financially and organizationally sustainable in the long term.

In the course of researching this book our team found that the term *strategy* is applied to organizational and programmatic questions such as those in the first list above, and also to operational challenges such as those in the second list. We also found that the term *strategic planning* is applied to most considerations of nonprofit strategy, whether they involve any actual planning or not. Again, since strategic planning is the only term of art our sector has for describing a consideration of strategy, it gets applied quite broadly, and as a result, is often misleading.

To manage the confusion that results from a single term playing so many different roles in the sector, I developed the Strategy Pyramid, which attempts to capture the full range of the sector's current use of the term by making distinctions between organizational, programmatic, and operational levels of strategy, and addressing each in turn. Before learning about the pyramid in Chapter 2, however, you need to understand the current state and limitations of nonprofit strategic planning. If you still question whether we need a nonprofit strategy revolution, read on.

The Disconnect Between Strategy and Strategic Planning

This book provides flexible and workable resources for the essential ongoing nonprofit task of forming and implementing strategies. I call this new approach *Real-Time Strategic Planning* because it encourages ongoing consideration of strategy as it is needed, not on a predetermined three-year cycle. Ironically, true strategy formation is not a role traditional strategic planning very often plays. In our research we most often heard strategic planning described by participants as a tool for team building. "It's a way to get everyone on the same page," several interviewees said. That is, strategic planning is intended for the setting of annual goals by work groups, and for communication of the leadership's intentions, rather than as a process to form, adjust, and implement the organizational strategies that will carry out those intentions. This purpose makes sense, since traditional strategic planning is better suited to team building than to the formation of strategy.

You can see this disconnect clearly in the distance between the far-reaching mission and vision statements embodied in many strategic plans and the relatively mundane goals that are established to advance them. For example, one organization's mission is to "end hunger in our community," but, after an environmental scan and several meetings of the strategic planning committee, staff, and board, it arrives at a set of goals that includes

1. Increase the diversity of our board of directors
2. Develop a new staff training program that raises the quality of our services
3. Investigate the possibility of and requirements for establishing an endowment fund

No doubt about it, these are important activities, but it is difficult to trace a direct path from these concerns to the advancement of the organization's mission. The mission is appropriately large, but the first two goals are too operational and the third is too tentative and ephemeral to be of much strategic use.

How does that disconnect arise? As La Piana Associates conducted research on nonprofit strategic planning, we began to uncover trends in such disconnects. Some of these problems result from the traditions surrounding the process of strategic planning, while others are inherent in the planning process itself. They are

- Mistaking goals for strategy
- Generating more goals than can reasonably be pursued
- Expecting strategies to fit within a rigid time line
- Confusing strategic planning with consensus building
- Forecasting the future from a snapshot in time
- Pretending to be objective
- Frustrating staff through bad data, inaction, or both

Let's look more closely at how a nonprofit could arrive at a strategic plan containing a set of goals so deeply disconnected from sound strategy that a mission to "end hunger in our community" is served by a strategy diffusely expressed as "investigate the possibility of and requirements for establishing an endowment fund."

Mistaking goals for strategy

No matter what resources you consult, books you read, or consultants you interview, you are likely to see a proposed process something like that outlined in Exhibit A, Traditional Strategic Planning (page 9). We'll call this process *traditional* strategic planning to emphasize that it has been done this way for a long time now. You can see from this linear and closed-ended process how a grand mission or vision can boil down to some pretty pedestrian goals and objectives. Perhaps you can also imagine how the goals and objectives are likely to be set. The process is earnest and well meaning, but flawed. The reason, quite plainly, if nonsensically, is that most often a consideration of strategy is absent from the strategic planning process. *When you focus on goal-setting rather than strategy formation you get goals that, while valuable in themselves, may not add up to anything bigger.*

EXHIBIT A Traditional Strategic Planning

Step 1: Plan to plan—make sure all stakeholders agree to a review of the nonprofit's mission and goals. Establish a budget and time frame for the process.

Step 2: Form a planning committee composed of key board and staff leaders.

Step 3: Decide whether to engage a consultant—and unless you are just doing a one-day strategic planning retreat, you will probably need one.

Step 4: Convene the committee for several meetings; go through the following process:

- Review and rewrite the mission statement—usually defined as the social good the nonprofit wants to create.
- Articulate a vision—usually defined as the future the nonprofit will create.
- Use surveys, interviews, focus groups, SWOT analysis, and Internet research to learn all about the nonprofit's external environment—profile competitors, describe client needs, identify demographic and funding trends, etc.
- From all the data that is gathered and sifted try to identify either:
  - Three critical issues you must address (the critical issues approach).
  - Four future scenarios that might occur (the scenarios approach).
  - Some other definable variables you think are important.

  This involves wide consultation among stakeholders because it is the point where, essentially, the organization says "This is what is important."

- Set goals for
  - Addressing each of the critical issues (if using that approach).
  - Board composition or performance (e.g., find four new members).
  - Programmatic performance (e.g., serve 400 people).
  - Financial management or performance (e.g., build a reserve).
  - Human resource management (e.g., reduce staff turnover by 50 percent).
  - Fundraising (e.g., increase annual giving by 10 percent).
  - Facilities (e.g., replace the roof next year before it rains).
  - Outcomes (e.g., 60 percent of clients will get better). Set dates by which each of the goals will be met.
- Develop three to five "action steps" or "objectives" for each goal.
- Set dates by which each of the objectives will be met.
- Assign responsible parties for each goal and objective.
- Draft the plan and include all the research in appendices.

Step 5: Share the draft with each stakeholder group, obtain feedback, and redraft as necessary to obtain near-consensus.

Step 6: Ask the board to approve the plan, covering the next three years. Print it, bind it nicely, and distribute it widely within the organization and to external stakeholders.

Generating more goals
than can reasonably be pursued

Exhibit A outlines eight standard "goal areas" (the newly identified critical issues, and the standard areas of concern: board, program, finances, human resources, fundraising, facilities, and outcomes). Other process models might suggest a larger or smaller number of areas, but eight will do for our example. Let's assume you need to set three goals per area—except, of course, for the program area where, if you have many programs, you might need more goals to cover them all. So let's estimate that in each of seven areas you set three goals (subtotal: twenty-one goals) and add to that number nine more goals in the program area (covering three programs), for a total of thirty goals. Now, each goal will need at least three action steps or objectives to carry it out. So in the end you will have set thirty goals and developed ninety action steps.

I am not exaggerating. We often encounter clients with previous strategic plans that count far more goals and objectives than these! Obviously, no one is going to be able to keep track of all these goals and objectives, much less work steadily on so many disparate issues at once. The result is either to pick and choose, or to ignore the document entirely.

Expecting strategies to fit within a rigid time line

As if this were not bad enough, something else happens that can render the entire process moot. The typical time frame for a strategic plan today seems to be three years. A decade ago it was five years. The problem with these multiyear projections is this: not only does the nonprofit set a long-term vision, but it tries to anticipate the goals and objectives needed over the next three years to get there. In practice, when I encounter a client with an existing strategic plan, I rarely find that most of the goals projected to be completed anywhere beyond the first year are still taken seriously by the board and staff. In our rapid-response world, it is just not possible to anticipate what will be important to work on (at that level of detail) years, or even one full year, in advance. Moreover, the more goals you set, the less crucial accomplishing each becomes.

Of course, traditional strategic planning is elastic. When we find that we are no longer pursuing our goals after the first year, we switch to setting only one year's worth of goals. We institute yearly check-ups in which we set the next year's goals and objectives, thus keeping the time frame for review shorter, while the overall vision remains intact.

This elasticity is good. Several years ago I dubbed this method "Fast Track Strategic Planning," because I was still trying to make traditional strategic planning work, only with a shorter time frame and a less intensive investment of my clients' resources. Still, many goals set in this way are too rigid or sound good at the time they are written but do not correspond to the reality on the ground a few short months later. I think it is safe to say that no more than 10 percent of all the goals set by nonprofits using a process like this are ever met.[14] Worse still, to my mind, probably fewer than half of all goals set in this way are even pursued in any seriousness.

Confusing strategic planning with consensus building

Take a moment to revisit Exhibit A. Unless you are new to nonprofits, you'll recognize the process. Step 5—review by stakeholders—is particularly dangerous, as any tentative decisions made during the process can be undone by the organization's stakeholder groups. Essentially, if you have decided to say no to any issue or group in the interest of gaining greater focus, conflict will inevitably arise. The well-meaning nonprofit drive for consensus can undermine difficult, but necessary, priority-setting decisions. The danger inherent in Step 5 is directly tied to what so many nonprofits cite as the reason for strategic planning: that it is a good way to "get everyone on the same page."

While understanding the impact of strategy on constituents is vital, seeking consensus can in fact be damaging, such as when the organization is stymied: unable to reach consensus, yet equally unable to move forward without it. This weakness in traditional strategic planning could best be described as *unity seeking*. While reaching consensus or even unanimity can be strategically helpful, it is not a good reason in itself to form strategies, but rather a by-product of a good strategic process.

---

[14] I did not pick the 10 percent figure out of thin air. Some years ago a business study revealed that only 10 percent of strategies adopted by corporations were deemed successful. Commenting on this report, management guru Tom Peters (author of *In Search of Excellence*) said that figure was "wildly exaggerated!" (Rod Napier, Clint Sidle, and Patrick Sanaghan, *High Impact Tools and Activities for Strategic Planning: Creative Techniques for Facilitating Your Organization's Planning Process* [New York: McGraw-Hill, 1996], 1.)

Forecasting the future from a snapshot in time

Strategic planning, as currently practiced, requires a nonprofit to devote adequate resources to researching various aspects of its external environment (aka its market). This process is usually referred to in traditional strategic planning as the "market research study" or the "environmental scan." This is an expensive and time-consuming process, often especially beyond the reach of grassroots or otherwise resource-thin organizations. It is equally unappealing to groups that need to move quickly or that are in an especially dynamic, rapid-response environment, and to those needing to be more nimble in developing strategies for moving ahead. The environmental scan, usually done at the outset of the process, is often quite broad and poorly focused: "Tell us what people think of our organization, what our strengths and weaknesses are, and what opportunities we should pursue next" is a common starting place handed to consultants. Unless those consultants take the time to contextualize the work, that is, to focus it on the issues most pertinent to this organization at this time, the results of this undertaking can be both broad and shallow.

Often, an environmental scan of any depth or size is conducted by independent consultants who bring their own methodology and pace to the process. While consultants also bring expertise and neutrality to traditional strategic planning, outsourcing the environmental scan in toto does not help the organization learn how to conduct its own on-the-ground market research—an important element in building its internal capacity to think and act strategically on an ongoing basis.

A strategy engagement with Peninsula Open Space Trust (POST), a highly regarded land trust located just south of San Francisco, which recently completed a $200,000,000 capital campaign to fund land acquisitions, asked "What's next?" Throughout this engagement our client acted as a team with the consultants, both determining the precise questions to be answered by the market research, and increasingly, as the process unfolded, doing the research themselves. Walter T. Moore, executive vice president of POST, spearheaded the process. He says: "We did not start off with an environmental scan, but worked it into the process once we were underway and were able to focus it more narrowly on our specific needs. Even then, by the end of the process, we were doing the work ourselves. The consultants were resources for us, and helped us make sense of what we learned, but by largely doing the scan ourselves we also learned a skill we will use long into the future."

Finally, the very act of undertaking an environmental scan presupposes that the organization's world will remain relatively stable, or at least that the changes it will experience are foreseeable. Otherwise, the environmental scan is nothing more than a snapshot in time: this is how the world looks to us today. This is useful intelligence in the short term, but problematic for a three-year plan. In dynamic and unpredictable environments, such as we regularly experience across the sector, the forward-looking environmental scan may quickly become a glance in the rearview mirror.

Remember how the Central Intelligence Agency (CIA) discovered that the Soviet Union was in collapse? Despite all the billions of dollars the U.S. government spent keeping tabs on its prime foe, CIA officials watched the Berlin Wall coming down on CNN, just like the rest of us. That should give you reason to pause as you consider investing a few thousand dollars every three years in an effort to understand the complex world your nonprofit lives in right now.

Karl Weick, author of *Sensemaking in Organizations,* drives the point home, saying, "The dominance of retrospect in sensemaking is a major reason why students of sensemaking find forecasting, contingency planning, strategic planning, and other magical probes into the future wasteful and misleading if they are decoupled from reflective action and history."[15]

Making sense of the world around us is a prime goal of all strategic thinking. But, as Weick points out, we make sense of our world in retrospect, having lived through the events of the day—not in advance, as we try to predict coming events without understanding their context. Triennial market research by consultants may provide some clues to the future, but, as Weick suggests, sensemaking requires more: the organization itself must be deeply engaged, on an ongoing basis, in understanding its current situation and its history to have any hope of forecasting the future.

And thus the problem with forecasting in traditional strategic planning: forecasts, meant to shape strategy for three years, are derived from a present-day snapshot, often taken by photographers—external market researchers—with cursory knowledge of their subject nonprofit and little sense of its historical context. Good forecasting, for strategic purposes, requires constant attention to the present, informed by a strong sense of history and a close connection to the failed and successful outcomes of strategies informed by previous forecasts. Such predictions are best made by the people who will experience firsthand the consequences of their forecasts.

---

[15] Karl E. Weick, *Sensemaking in Organizations* (Thousand Oaks, CA: Sage Publications, 1995), 30.

Pretending to be objective

Let's turn to another popular tool of traditional strategic planning, the Strengths, Weaknesses, Opportunities, and Threats, or "SWOT" analysis. No other process or tool is so closely identified with strategic planning as this one. In fact, I have heard strategic planning referred to as SWOT, as in the request "Can you facilitate a SWOT for us?" Despite the evident uniqueness of every nonprofit I have encountered, in my experience, the strengths and weaknesses or "SW" portions of almost every SWOT analysis I have seen are essentially the same. Participants typically say things like those contained in the short list in Exhibit B, Typical Strength/Weakness Results.

EXHIBIT B Typical Strength/Weakness Results

Strengths	Weaknesses
We have a great leader (*Boilerplate: Every nonprofit says this*)	*I have never seen:* We have a weak leader
We have a talented and dedicated staff (*Boilerplate: Every nonprofit says this*)	*I have never seen:* We have terrible staff
We have a stellar board	We could use a stronger board
We have great cash flow	We have a cash flow problem
We have a great reputation	No one knows who we are
Our clients love us	Our clients are impossible to please

The list goes on and on but you get the idea: platitudes and statements of the obvious. This exercise could almost be done using a checklist of about fifty choices. It is difficult to get at any depth, and especially at any unpleasant but necessary-to-discuss truths, using this superficial process in a group setting with internal stakeholders. Nonetheless, it is an essential part of most traditional nonprofit strategic planning processes.

On the other hand, the opportunities and threats or "OT" portion of the SWOT exercise may indeed bring to light real opportunities and dangerous threats. Perhaps it is because this part of the discussion is focused externally, where participants feel less responsibility for (and ownership of) the results. Because they are externally focused, it is also true that their honest comments ("ABC seems to be encroaching on our clientele") may be less likely to hurt their colleagues' feelings, and thus to endanger their own position, than, for example, saying, during the SW portion of the exercise, "Our executive director stinks." Still, when the OT results are presented in the form of the inevitable list or table, and then juxtaposed with the generally meaningless platitudes that comprise the SW list, most groups fail to take any actionable meaning away from the exercise. This is a shame, since making meaning (sensemaking, in Weick's terminology) that can result in organizational behavior change is what strategy is ultimately all about.

Even bringing in outside stakeholders (clients, funders, referral sources, partners, and so forth) to sit in on the meetings does not always counter the strong tendency of the SWOT group process toward SW platitudes. It would be very difficult, not to mention socially awkward, for anyone to sit in a meeting with an ineffective executive director and declare to the group that "A lack of leadership is a major weakness."

Frustrating staff through bad data, inaction, or both

So far, we've seen that traditional strategic planning relies on processes and traditions that confuse goals with strategy, force fit strategies to a specific time line, favor unity over strategy, employ ineffective forecasting, and often lack the objectivity to uncover true strengths and weaknesses. These and other limitations of traditional strategic planning, which I first noticed as a young executive director in the early 1980s, have become ever more apparent to me in the course of more than a decade as a consultant helping scores of nonprofits to develop their plans.

These are vulnerabilities in traditional strategic planning, but they can be overcome by using good processes and good consulting. It is not as though the strategic plans that so many nonprofits have developed have been useless. However, there are fundamental problems with traditional strategic planning. That is why reform won't do—why we need a nonprofit strategy revolution. The worst of these difficulties—we might collectively call them the *casus belli,* the causes of the revolution—are (1) overreliance on underreliable data, (2) time delays that put the organization on hold and result in inaction, and ultimately (3) the frustration of the very staff and volunteers who must act on the strategies.

1. Overreliance on underreliable data

My daughters Marisa and Tessa were the perfect target market demographic at the height of the Beanie Baby boom of the 1990s. One of the arguments they made—as grade-schoolers no less!—for buying more of these stuffed animals was, as Marisa, then nine years old, put it: "They'll be worth something someday." I didn't really believe it; still we bought lots of Beanie Babies, some of which came with protective clear plastic dust covers like the one my mother used to put on the statue of the Virgin Mary in my parents' bedroom.

As Exhibit C, Beanie Baby Mania (below) demonstrates, bad data, a changing world, or just plain wishful thinking can lead to mistaken predictions. Unfortunately the consequences are often far more disastrous than an attic full of small, cute, and all-but-worthless stuffed toys. This problem of bad data or poor forecasting sounds like the problem with environmental scans, discussed above. But it is deeper than that. It is a fundamentally flawed belief that good data, if it is available, will yield good strategy. Most nonprofits mistakenly believe that if they ask the right questions on a regular three-year cycle, they can predict major demographic or market shifts, and then figure

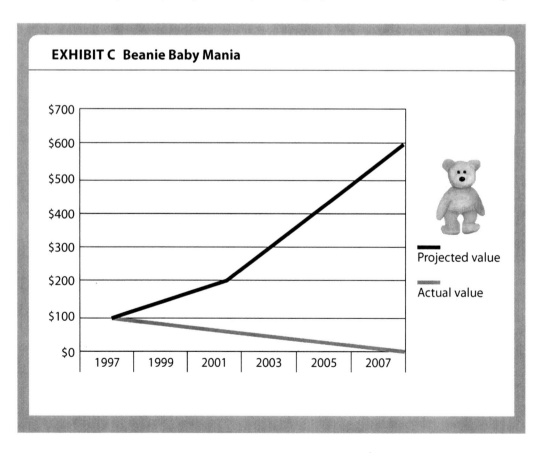

EXHIBIT C Beanie Baby Mania

Projected value

Actual value

out what to do about them in a timely way, thus enabling the nonprofit to set goals that will bring success in the future. In practice it seldom works out that way. In place of occasional concerted attempts to foretell major changes in their future environment, nonprofits need to continuously scan and engage with their environment as part of their strategic efforts. Current planning puts too much distance between prediction and action.

2. Time delays put organization on hold

Just as traditional strategic planning distances prediction from action, it puts too much time between strategic thinking and action. A nonprofit typically requires six to twelve months (or longer) to complete its strategic planning process. In fact, the David and Lucile Packard Foundation conducted a study in 2006 which revealed that the average length of time for a strategic planning process supported by an organizational effectiveness grant from the foundation was fourteen months,[16] which is certainly inadequate to address the demands of a rapid-response world. During this time it is often difficult for the organization's leaders to respond to emerging opportunities or challenges, as their strategic thinking energy is bound up in the ongoing strategic planning process and, until it is concluded, they have no "direction." They may thus be immobilized by concern that any new commitments the organization makes will be out of line with the official strategic direction, which, of course, has yet to emerge from the planning process. The organization may come to feel as though it is "on hold," unable to move until its strategic plan is completed. Such hesitation can be costly, particularly when the organization takes a pass on stellar opportunities that require action.

"I don't know whether we should jump at one or both of these opportunities. Our strategic planning process is just getting started," said Ruth Bolan, a participant in an executive director leadership program that I was leading. She directed O'hia Productions, a unique "local-style" children's theater in Hawai'i that had been offered both the possibility of providing the Christmas entertainment at the state's largest shopping center for the next five years and, in an entirely separate situation, a contract to provide drama activities for kids with the state's largest child care provider. During a break we discussed how strategic opportunities such as these do not automatically follow the completion of a strategic planning process. In fact, it was darn inconvenient of them to turn up now, at the very outset of that process. I asked Ruth two questions: What was her sense of the fit of each of these

---

[16] Stephanie McAuliffe, director, The David and Lucile Packard Foundation, in remarks at the Council of Foundations' annual conference, 7 May 2006, in a session we co-led titled *Strategic Planning: Less Than Meets the Eye?*

opportunities with her organization? What was the organization's capacity to carry off one or both of these new ventures *right now?* I heard back from her a week later. She studied the programs, ran the numbers, engaged her staff and board in discussions of what she had learned, and decided to go after both opportunities, greatly strengthening O'hia's financial position and widening its audience base. What's more, she did all of this *before* launching her strategic planning process.

Exhibit D, The Planning-Doing Cycle (page 19) depicts the difference between the requirements of traditional strategic planning and the real strategy needs of nonprofits. As Ruth Bolan learned, the reality of nonprofit life requires a faster, continuous cycle of strategic thinking and action as portrayed in the second graphic, not a separation of organizational life into reflective and active periods, as the first graphic implies.

Moreover, planning is, of necessity, usually carried out by a select group of board members and managers, with at best token representation from frontline staff. Yet the plan, if it is to succeed, must be embraced and implemented throughout the organization, typically by many individuals who had little involvement in its creation, and who thus may have little stake in its success. In *Good to Great*, Jim Collins suggests that prior to charting an organizational direction, it is critical to first "get the right people on the bus, and the wrong people off the bus."[17] In other words, strategy is the result of the work of a group of people—hopefully the "right" group. He offers compelling evidence that processes such as strategic planning may not be as effective as generally thought in producing results, particularly as regards building the culture of success and can-do spirit that are essential to entrepreneurial nonprofits.

Nonprofits need processes that are inclusive, that make people want to jump on the bus, and that allow every voice to be heard in discussions of the bus's destination. Yet nonprofits also need to make decisions, which means to achieve greater focus they sometimes have to say no to valued ideas backed by solid constituencies. They also need to stick with a course of action until it either achieves success or is determined to be less workable than another alternative. These dual ends—engagement and action—are best accomplished through continual processes, where organizational stakeholders come to believe that their input is truly important and always needed, not just once every three years through strategic planning focus groups whose proceedings seem to have little bearing on the organization's life.

---

[17] Jim Collins, *Good to Great: Why Some Companies Make the Leap . . . and Others Don't* (New York: Harper Business, 2001), 21.

EXHIBIT D The Planning-Doing Cycle

Traditional planning:
Long, discrete, and separated from the external environment

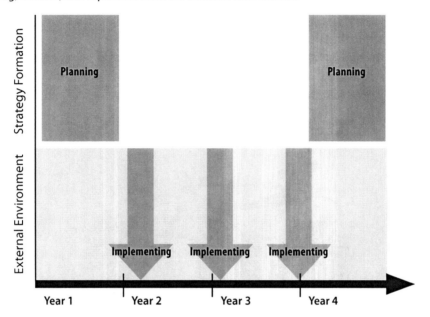

Reality:
Nonprofits need ongoing strategic thinking and acting in the context of the environment

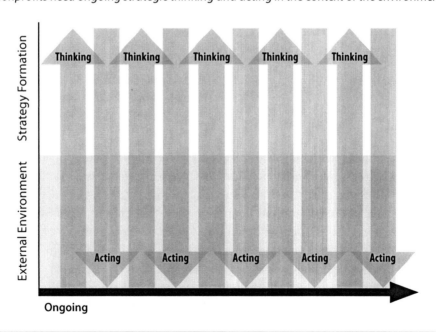

Many nonprofit executives, on the other hand, find that their performance assessment is tied to the accomplishment of very specific goals as articulated in a strategic plan. This admirable attempt at accountability by nonprofit boards can result in nonprofit leaders working very hard to accomplish goals that have become less important than addressing newly emerging opportunities. The overly specific goals that result from most strategic plans may even be rendered irrelevant by shifts in the organization's environment. In such situations, strategic planning can be more detrimental than helpful, causing nonprofits to lose valuable time, expend scarce resources, and divert their attention from higher-value activities.

3. Frustration of staff and volunteers

After fifty years of careful research and planning, Ernest, Leonard, and Victor were ecstatic about finishing their strategy for winning triathlon competitions.

Perhaps the most pernicious effect of traditional strategic planning is that it wears out the participants just when the game is supposed to begin. They are either frustrated and disappointed at the lack of action or are in awe of the voluminous document they have created. Either way, they are "done." Thus, the traditional three-year strategic planning cycle sends exactly the wrong message: that the process was about producing a document rather than about changing the organization. Participants, after endless months of strategic planning, may be forgiven for offering a collective sigh: "At least that's out of the way for the next three years!" Instead, as we shall see, continuous, responsive consideration of strategic challenges is the path to timely, successful strategic decision making and actions.

Of course, the work usually associated with strategic planning has merit. However, it must be understood in a more useful context. Recall the example of the organization with the mission to "end hunger in our community." The mission is at a suitably lofty level, and some of the organization's goals could be acted upon. Yet, this strategic formulation misses, oddly, strategy. If you could deploy a process that focuses clearly on forming strategy, then much of the work that is currently devoted to strategic planning could still be undertaken; however, it would be aimed at *operationalizing* the strategic thinking that must precede it, not *replacing* it with operational goals and objectives that are most often not implemented.

Finally, there is the too-frequent outcome that a strategic plan, after all the time and money spent on its completion, simply fails to make any significant difference in the organization's life. The standard phrase is that the plan "sits on a shelf gathering dust." This is more than a colossal waste of resources in itself (and I don't mean just shelf space); it also serves to blunt the organization's appetite for any future strategy work. "If we have to go through that again any time soon, I'll quit" is the oft-heard, desperate plea. This is perhaps the most unfortunate result of all, because forming strategy is an ongoing process—it affects everything. By making it into a triennial slog through a swamp of petty details, the nonprofit both wastes its leaders' energy and dulls their appetite for the real struggle to find and implement effective strategies. There has to be a better way, a way to engage nonprofits in forming strategies that work in real time—when they're needed.

Let me conclude this chapter with a quote from Henry Mintzberg, who is characteristically straightforward:

> Strategic thinking . . . is about synthesis. It involves intuition and creativity. The outcome of strategic thinking is an integrated perspective of the enterprise, a not-too-precisely articulated vision of direction. . . . Such strategies often cannot be developed on schedule and immaculately conceived. They must be free to appear at any time and at any place in the organization, typically through messy processes of informal learning that must necessarily be carried out by people at various levels who are deeply involved with the specific issues at hand.[18]

---

[18] Henry Mintzberg, "The Fall and Rise of Strategic Planning," *Harvard Business Review* (January-February 1994): 107–14 [adapted from Henry Mintzberg, *The Rise and Fall of Strategic Planning* (New York: Free Press, 1994), 108].

Conclusion: **Hence the Revolution**

Many of the process and practice problems I have described are regularly dealt with and overcome by the skills and experience of good strategic planners, whether they are consultants, experienced leaders, or just "naturals" at strategy. But nonprofits need a *system* that responds to today's rapidly changing environment and that does not require clever workarounds like "fast track strategic planning." Nonprofits should not have to rely on finding an especially skillful consultant to avoid some of the worst time- and energy-wasting aspects of current strategic planning practice. Fortunately, good strategic thinking is available to all nonprofit leaders, right there in their own heads and in the heads of their colleagues. They just need a better system in which to undertake it.

Disconnected and unreliable data, the long time lag, and the sheer draining quality of unending months of process combine to doom most traditional strategic plans to a space in the storeroom. You say you want a revolution? In the next chapter you will meet the Strategy Pyramid, a device for understanding the types and levels of strategic considerations your nonprofit faces. This concept will provide a context for our upcoming discussion of revolutionary new approaches to strategy.

Chapter Two:
The Strategy Pyramid

**If you can't describe what you are doing as a process,
you do not know what you are doing.**
—W. Edwards Deming[19]

THROUGH OUR RESEARCH and interviews with dozens of strategy theorists, nonprofit leaders, and consultants, I realized there is a need for a common language when talking about strategy.[20] Toward this end I devised the Strategy Pyramid[SM] as a system or organizing tool that helps us to think about categories of nonprofit strategy. In this chapter I introduce the Strategy Pyramid and explain the simple and straightforward process of using this structure to describe nonprofit strategy. The Strategy Pyramid is indeed a system[21] and it can indeed be described as a process, as Deming, the great management guru, requires: a system that works to provide a nonprofit with the elements of strategic thinking and action it requires.

The Strategy Pyramid is pictured in Exhibit E (see page 26). It is a simple graphic representation of the categories or types of challenges that confront the leaders of nonprofit organizations. Beginning at the pyramid's base, operations and **operational strategy** are concerned with routine administrative processes and management systems, and also with planning for future administrative needs. A sound operational infrastructure allows an

---

[19] W. Edwards Deming as quoted at http://en.thinkexist.com/quotes/
W._Edwards_Deming/.

[20] For a complete report on our strategy research process, see our online publication "The Strategy Formation Project," www.lapiana.org/consulting/research/sf.html.

[21] Per *Merriam-Webster's Collegiate Dictionary,* 11th ed. (2003), a system is "a regularly interacting or interdependent group of items forming a unified whole."

organization to develop a **programmatic strategy** and so to offer one or more programs, which are developed using the staff's (paid or voluntary) unique capabilities within the context of available resources and the organization's culture and values. Most of a nonprofit's resources are dedicated to its programs. At the **organizational strategy** level, big-picture issues about the organization, starting with its mission and vision, are addressed within an ongoing effort to assess trends in the environment and marketplace, and with an awareness of other actors in the nonprofit's market.

Aligning Organizational, Programmatic, and Operational Decisions

The Strategy Pyramid represents the successful resolution of often mundane but essential operational challenges as a necessary base upon which to build the organization. Programmatic decisions—determining how best to advance the mission—rest upon this successful base of operations. Organizational strategies that determine the nonprofit's market position and success at acquiring resources rest on its programs at the top of the pyramid. Thus we have a pyramid, with each level of organizational building blocks supported by what is, ideally, a solid and wider base underneath.

However appealing from a civil engineering standpoint this bottom-up approach to strategy formation might be, this particular pyramid is actually best built from the top down. First you determine mission, vision, and desired market position, which inform your organizational strategies and your choice of programmatic approaches. These in turn dictate the operational requirements of the entire enterprise.

For example, consider a nonprofit with a mission to defend the rights of immigrants. It needs to know who else is working in this area, what resources are available, and the most promising approaches to the problem. It needs also to understand its own unique contribution to the field. These deliberations will result in programmatic choices: for example, deciding to file lawsuits on behalf of individual immigrants, or to work with Congress to pass new immigration laws, or to run a public education media campaign to lessen anti-immigrant prejudice. These programmatic choices will in turn dictate the kind of organization that is needed to support them.

Will it want offices in areas around the country with high concentrations of immigrants (to identify immigrants in need of legal representation), or in Washington, DC (to facilitate its public policy work), or in New York or Los Angeles (for the media work)? Programmatic choices will also determine whether the organization hires a staff primarily composed of lawyers, of lobbyists and advocates, or of media relations people, and thus what kind of culture it will form.

As a practical matter, we seldom think of these issues as completely open choices, because we usually come into an existing organization as a staff member, board member, executive director, or consultant, and find that many of these decisions—the type of programs to be offered, staff to be hired, locations to be pursued, culture to be nurtured—have long since been made, either explicitly or implicitly. But even so, it is useful to begin a consideration of a nonprofit's strategy at the top of the pyramid with organizational strategies, and then to look for alignment with these top-level strategies, first among the organization's programmatic choices and then in its operations. Once this process is complete, ongoing implementation, review, and update of organizational, programmatic, and operational strategies can begin at any level. If the organization is not aligned top to bottom, then the pyramid is not well built and the mission, which sits at its apex, is subject to collapse.

Where's the Revolution?

With all the confusion around the term *strategy,* we have developed a unified definition that aligns the highest considerations of nonprofit leaders (mission, vision) with programmatic choices and operational systems and processes. This definition reflects what the better nonprofit leaders actually try to do with strategic planning. It brings much-needed clarity and comprehensibility to this essential but often-confusing concept of strategy. Nonprofit leaders who realize that strategy is more than a buzzword are able to develop and recognize true strategies— organized patterns of action that dramatically increase the success of their organizations. The revolution? We may hear the word strategy less, but see it in practice more.

EXHIBIT E   The Strategy Pyramid

ORGANIZATIONAL
Determine mission, vision,
trends, competitors, partners,
and market position

PROGRAMMATIC
Decide on approaches and offer programs and
activities to achieve specific outcomes related to the
target audiences

OPERATIONAL
Administer and oversee systems, policies, and personnel in areas such as
finance, human resources, communications, and information technology

Strategies can be formed at any of the three levels. Beginning at the base:

Operational strategies are aimed at enhancing a nonprofit's administrative efficiency, preparedness, and execution. Examples include

- A new model for staff training
- A long-range plan for repair and replacement of the physical plant as it ages
- Integrating a new technology into the programmatic work, such as the use of a web site

Programmatic strategies are intended to increase programmatic impact. Examples include

- A new approach to the work that promises better results at lower costs
- A new type of work that will better address the problem
- A new way of thinking about the problem

Organizational strategies help the nonprofit to garner resources of all kinds as it pursues its mission. Examples include

- A merger with the biggest competitor in the market
- An effort to appeal to more funders by becoming the most responsive player
- An offering of services in a new geographic location in order to attract new clients

In an ideal nonprofit organization, the strategies align from bottom to top to produce outcomes that achieve the organization's mission.

Successful Strategies Embody Implementation

The adage "execution trumps strategy" is indeed largely true in the non-profit world, as it is in business. A good, solid strategy, widely embraced and well implemented, is more likely to produce its intended result than is a far more brilliant stroke that is never operationalized because it is poorly understood by the staff who must implement it, unsupported by the board, or half-heartedly implemented by resistant managers. Successful strategies contain their own implementation plan. At the operational and programmatic levels they may look like the goals we all know from traditional strategic planning, but are often bigger, requiring a coordinated set of actions. Here are examples related to each level of the Strategy Pyramid.

Operational strategies

- To keep our staff's skills on the cutting edge we will fully implement the new "Gee Whiz" staff training model, over the next twelve months, at a cost of $20,000. Guillermo, our human resources director, will oversee.

- We will develop a plan for repair and replacement of the roof, boiler, and other key systems in our building over the next twenty years, and we will create a sinking fund to provide for these needs. Joan, our facilities manager, will coordinate with Sally, our chief financial officer.

- We will develop a new intranet to improve communications across departments. Anushka, our technology director, will oversee implementation and training.

Programmatic strategies

- Beginning in January, we will offer family therapy to supplement our clients' individual counseling. This has been shown to accelerate treatment and thus to shorten its duration while improving outcomes. Maria, our clinical director, will ensure that staff have the training to make this shift and will report initial results within six months.

- Within a year, we will integrate satellite and computer mapping into our wetlands preservation efforts to more closely monitor their status. Hugo, our computer whiz, will provide the technical support, and Lisa, our program director, will oversee the move online.

- By the end of the year we will hire two lawyers and begin offering legal services to our clients as well as emergency shelter and counseling. Maykao, our executive director, will manage this.

As you can see, operational and programmatic strategies resemble traditional strategic planning goals. However, at the organizational level, strategies are quite different. This is because traditional strategic planning tends to focus on operational and programmatic concerns, not organizational strategies. At the organizational level, strategies tend to be more complex, while still containing direction for their own implementation. Three examples follow.

Organizational strategies

- We will immediately pursue negotiations toward a merger with Big, Bad, and Ugly, our biggest competitor, to solidify our dominant position in the market and eliminate them as a competitive challenger. Mark, our CEO, will lead a team of board members in this effort. If negotiations fail, we will devise a new strategy for successful head-to-head competition, as we cannot just ignore them.

- We will form a market research team composed of board members and staff from throughout the organization to continuously study our market and thus to keep us abreast of the most likely developments in our field. Dasheka, our CEO, will facilitate the meetings, which will begin next month.

- After studying the market and running the numbers, we will rent a space in Fairlands, a community adjacent to our current location, hire staff, and begin operations by July 1. Opening this new office will double our potential market, and there appear to be no competitors in Fairlands. Janice, our CEO, and Bill, our program director, will coordinate this growth initiative.

Conclusion: **A Framework to Fuel Change**

The Strategy Pyramid is a tool for thinking about categories of strategy, that is, the types of concerns that exist at different levels throughout the organization. It is also a tool for understanding the relationships among the different levels of strategic thinking and decisions that are needed in any organization. It offers a new clarity and the framework upon which the nonprofit strategy revolution will be built. To use this framework we will need tools and processes for developing and implementing strategies that will help nonprofits to succeed, building an ongoing capacity to think and act strategically throughout the organization.

A cornerstone of our revolution is that *organizational strategy comes first.* We will focus on organizational strategy in the next two chapters.

Chapter Three:
Understanding Organizational Strategy

The future doesn't just happen—it's shaped by decisions.
> –Paul Tagliabue, former commissioner,
> National Football League[22]

Mission, Competitive Advantage, and Strategy

To be in control of your nonprofit's future, you must ask and answer the question: How will we accomplish our mission? The answers you give to this question vary in different contexts and at different times, but should articulate *organizational strategies*, the part of strategy concerned with the topmost portion of the Strategy Pyramid. Building on the generic definition offered in Chapter 1 (strategy is a coordinated set of actions toward an end), let's define strategy in

ORGANIZATIONAL
Determine mission, vision, trends, competitors, partners, and market position

a *nonprofit* context as "a coordinated set of actions aimed at creating and sustaining a competitive advantage in carrying out the nonprofit mission."

Now let's take this definition apart piece by piece.

---

22 Paul Tagliabue, as quoted by Christopher Tkaczyk at http://money.cnn.com/magazines/fortune/fortune_archive/2005/12/12/8363106/index.htm.

A coordinated set of actions . . . Strategy is about *action.* To be sure, it begins with thinking, discussing, discerning, and yes, some degree of planning; but it is not strategy unless all this cerebral effort is ultimately expressed in good old-fashioned action. Organizations constantly undertake a wide array of activities: delivering services, managing finances, supervising staff, raising money, recruiting board members, and many more. The list of nonprofit activities is, as you well know, endless. But unless the organization's key actions are coordinated—that is, unless they are pulling the organization in the same direction, toward the same ends—you do not have strategy. In fact, when a nonprofit's actions are not coordinated, what you quite often have is either inertia or total chaos.

. . . aimed at creating and sustaining a competitive advantage . . . The concept of *competitive advantage* is borrowed from the business world, where it is used a bit differently than here. La Piana Associates' definition of strategy is based on the McKinsey & Company definition of business strategy, adapted by us for the nonprofit context. McKinsey's definition is "A *strategy* is an integrated set of actions designed to create sustainable competitive advantage."[23] The essential truth remains in both the business and nonprofit sectors—the purpose of strategy is to create competitive advantage where none exists and to strengthen competitive advantage where it does exist. In the nonprofit world, *competitive advantage* can be defined, from the viewpoint of the customer, as the presence of visible, obvious, and measurable ways in which your organization differs from and is better than its peers.

Where's the Revolution?

Traditional strategic planning is about setting goals and creating a plan to achieve them, but real strategy is about taking action in real time. Remember the old children's riddle: Five frogs sat on a log. One decided to jump off, so how many are left? The right answer is not four but five— there is a big difference between *deciding to jump* and actually *taking the leap.**

* Mark L. Feldman and Michael F. Spratt, *Five Frogs on a Log: A CEO's Field Guide to Accelerating the Transition in Mergers, Acquisitions, and Gut Wrenching Change* (New York: HarperCollins, 1999).

---

[23] Kevin P. Coyne, "The Anatomy of Sustainable Competitive Advantage," *McKinsey Quarterly* 2 (Spring 1986): 50–65.

Customers is a blanket term to cover all people with whom your organization makes exchanges: retail customers, clients, donors, potential board members, staff members, or the public at large.

This leads to the last part of the definition.

. . . in carrying out the nonprofit mission. In the corporate world, the concept of competitive advantage refers to aspects of the business model or strategy that make it difficult or (preferably) impossible for competitors to enter or remain in the market. In the nonprofit world, the term suggests a different end. The "visible, obvious and measurable ways in which one organization is different from and performs better than its peers" are only of value if they directly advance the organization's mission. For example, one organization might clearly have a lower-cost program than its competitors, but if it achieves that cost savings through ineffective program design, understaffing, or delivering poor or inconsistent quality, then its lower cost is not a competitive advantage. It may be cheaper, but it is not better. On the other hand, an organization whose costs are in the same ballpark as its peers, but produces superior outcomes through its program design, staff motivation and skill, or other distinctive features, has a true differentiating, competitive advantage.

And that's when Squeaks and Jerry realized that
Mr. Scampers really did have a competitive advantage.

Competitive advantage is all about differentiation. Funders complain about duplication in the nonprofit sector because they see many organizations trying to address the same problem in pretty much the same way (from their perspective, at least). Differences between your nonprofit and its competitors may loom large in your staff's minds, but from the distance of the funder perspective, the programs appear to be identical. During my days running a nonprofit serving emotionally disturbed children, there were huge philosophical differences between the professional staffs of neighboring agencies. One nonprofit swore by a behavioral approach, another believed that a family systems orientation worked best, and my staff was devoted to a psychodynamic perspective. From the viewpoint of these mental health professionals, the differing approaches represented gaping chasms of difference, but our common funder, the public mental health authority, neither noticed nor cared. All it wanted was results. Even I had to admit—after getting to know our competitors—that we all seemed to work with kids in the same commonsense ways. What differed was how each of the staffs talked about their work at the end of their day.

Regardless of the scale of the need or the skill of the organizations addressing the problem, the funder perception of duplication persists—and remember, customer perception is what counts in competitive advantage. Consider, for example, a community that has one thousand homeless people. There are five independently operated homeless shelters, each with a fifty-bed capacity. At full capacity, the entire shelter system can only serve 25 percent of the need. Nonetheless, many donors and other customers (legislators, policymakers, voters) will see five shelters and complain of inefficient duplication of effort. As a result they may be less interested in supporting any of the five. Indeed the field may be inefficient, but not because of duplication; rather, it is so because of a lack of scale.

While the individual homeless shelters could argue that more funding and shelters are needed, the best way to address this funder concern about the perceived duplication of effort may be for strong nonprofits to separate themselves from the pack by demonstrating better outcomes. These constitute a competitive advantage leading to differentiation in the donor's mind, and eventually to more resources. Greater resources will enable those that produce superior outcomes to reach a larger number of clients.

I will further discuss competitive advantage later, including how to identify, promote, and strengthen yours.

Where's the Revolution?

We were amazed to learn that not a single organization among the twenty-five in our pilot cohorts had ever held an in-depth discussion of competitive advantage in its prior strategic planning efforts. Nor had most of them given much organized thought to their competition. Generally, they found this analysis to be extremely helpful to understanding their market position. As one pilot organization executive director said, "We have continued to think about our competition. . . . We have one competitor that is definitely the 800-pound gorilla in the field . . . and we began to ask ourselves why we are creating this organization when the competitor is already so well established in this area. We have continued to think about that and we have developed an answer—one that I increasingly use when I am talking with funders and others who ask me about our mission."

What Is Organizational Strategy?

In discussing the Strategy Pyramid in Chapter 2 we learned that nonprofits can consider strategy at three levels—organizational, programmatic, and operational. The latter two are treated separately in Chapters 7 and 8, respectively. However, any overall consideration of nonprofit strategy must begin at the top, with organization-level strategy.

Organizational strategy is the means a nonprofit uses to determine how it will advance its mission, realize it vision, and deliver real value to the community or cause it serves, through successfully navigating competitive, collaborative, and other market dynamics. If operational strategy is concerned with how the nonprofit is run on a daily basis, and programmatic strategy with how the nonprofit's programmatic activity will meet real needs in the most effective way, *organizational strategy is about who and what the nonprofit is in the larger world.* It is about organizational identity, direction, brand, and market position. It is also about the nonprofit's relationships, both competitive and collaborative, with other entities, whether for-profit, public, or nonprofit.

A nonprofit exists in a world filled with other actors that can be either collaborators, competitors, or both. To succeed, the nonprofit continually monitors its environment, assesses future trends, and either consciously carves out, or unconsciously falls into, a position relative to others in its market. It develops relationships with supporters of all kinds as it continuously works to acquire sufficient resources to pursue its mission. It must ask itself questions such as

- What is our mission—the change we seek to achieve in the world?
- What is our organization's role in realizing its vision for the world?
- What social, political, economic, technological, and environmental trends affect us?
- How do we attract all the different resources we need to advance our mission?
- What Big Questions (our term for strategic challenges) are we currently facing?

These are the same concerns that drive traditional strategic planning. The revolutionary difference is not in the challenges you face or even in the types of questions that you ask. In traditional strategic planning, questions—about the external environment, competitors and collaborators, and Big Questions—are addressed, if at all, in a formal way and only once

---

Where's the Revolution?

Mission, vision, environment, resource procurement, and Big Questions are all drivers of traditional strategic planning. So, how is what we're proposing revolutionary? Two ways: First, in our model, these dynamics are regularly explored (sometimes continuously and sometimes intermittently, depending on conditions). Because strategic crises and opportunities don't conform to timetables, the organization (not an external consultant) continuously probes for such crises and opportunities. Second, the moment the organization identifies changed dynamics (that is, something new affecting mission, vision, resources, and so forth) it must form actionable strategies, not tactical goals. In our model, strategy suggests its own implementation. It is strategy that connects mission to goals.

every three years, regardless of when they arise. The revolutionary difference represented by Real-Time Strategic Planning is contained in two parts, one related to timing and the other to the translation between mission, strategy, and goals.

First, Real-Time Strategic Planning requires the organization to consider the factors listed above on an ongoing basis, addressing them as needed. In some cases the organization faces the factors more or less continuously, while in others it does so intermittently. Organizational strategy cannot be developed and implemented successfully on a predetermined strategic planning timetable. Because crises and opportunities cannot be scheduled, anticipation of and response to them cannot be set on a three-year cycle. Nor can organizational strategy be outsourced to consultants; you must get down in the trenches and do a great deal of the research—and learning—yourself.

Second, Real-Time Strategic Planning requires that when you identify, understand, and have a strong grasp of how these dynamics will impact your organization, you must then form actual strategies to address them, not simply develop a series of goals. *Strategy connects your mission to your goals.* Ironically, as I noted earlier, it is most often missing from traditional strategic planning.

From Theory to Action:

Probing for Opportunities

Today's environment changes rapidly, and successful nonprofits must probe continuously for crises and opportunities that can necessitate the formation of new strategies. The following tools will help you to develop an ongoing capacity for strategic thinking and acting:

▶ Tool 14: Strategic Thinkers Group (on CD)

▶ Tool 16: Reading Group (on CD)

▶ Tool 17: Brainstorming Process (on CD)

▶ Tool 18: Scenario Thinking (on CD)

Most of these tools are neither new nor unique to this book. We are simply repurposing them. Instead of being stand-alone, one-time activities, they, and other tools you will find in the same section, can be pressed into service in the effort to build your organization's ability to anticipate and respond to strategic challenges and opportunities in your community.

What Does Organizational Strategy Look Like?

Organizational strategy consists of the actions you take to create and sustain a competitive advantage in carrying out your mission. A good strategy can be enduring and need not be adjusted on a predictable three-year planning cycle. Indeed, it may need to change only when it is no longer the best way to advance your mission; in other words, when it is no longer working optimally.

Here are two examples of enduring strategies.

The first is taken from the Oakland (California) Symphony in the 1980s. The challenge the symphony faced was a big, well-funded, and high-quality competitor just across the bay—the San Francisco Symphony. Living in the shadow of one of the nation's great symphonies was difficult. The symphony's Big Question was "How do we thrive in an environment dominated by the San Francisco Symphony?" The answer: the Oakland Symphony decided to change the rules of the game. Their strategy to accomplish this might be stated as follows:

> We will offer exceptionally well-performed new music not played by the San Francisco Symphony, and we will cater to a local audience. We will commission new works from prominent and rising contemporary composers, aiming consistently for a "wow" factor. We will keep our costs down through offering a fairly limited performance schedule. We will strive for a predictable income stream by aggressively seeking season subscriptions.

This strategy paid huge dividends for the Oakland Symphony. Led by Calvin Simmons, its dynamic young African American conductor, the symphony became known, just as it had sought to be, for new and exciting musical performances. In fact this strategy proved so successful that patrons began to come *from* San Francisco to hear the different music played across the bridge in Oakland. The Oakland Symphony had achieved musical (mission) success and market differentiation, and it did so by developing and consistently reinforcing its competitive advantage.

This basic organizational strategy worked well for many years. Then it began to unravel. The Oakland Symphony embraced a new strategy, but one that was not well thought out. The board decided to begin a broader repertoire, aiming to be recognized as a national rather than a regional symphony. For the same reason, it expanded its performance schedule and as a consequence took in a smaller percentage of its revenue through season tickets. As a result, income became less predictable just when, because of program growth, cash flow would be most sorely tested. The beautiful and historic old Paramount Theatre, the symphony's home, was an expensive luxury, with high operating costs and constant maintenance needs. Then, tragically, Calvin Simmons died in a boating accident. In a matter of a few years the Oakland Symphony was bankrupt.[24]

A happier story, also from Oakland, is that of East Bay Agency for Children (EBAC), which I served as executive director for sixteen years. This is the organization (profiled earlier) with the "wish list" strategic plan stowed away among the mops and buckets (page 3). EBAC developed this organizational strategy during my tenure, and it continues to work well for the organization more than a decade after I departed. In 1982, EBAC was a very small nonprofit, serving just twenty emotionally troubled children in a single day-treatment program. Its competitors consisted of much larger organizations that possessed acres of land and extensive, although aging, physical plants, within which they offered both day treatment and very expensive twenty-four-hour residential care for troubled children. EBAC could not attract the community's philanthropic attention at the small scale where it was stuck and, as a forty-year-old organization, time was running out. EBAC's Big Question was "How can we compete with the well-established and better-funded organizations we currently find in our market?" Another way of stating this Big Question might be "How can we best serve the community given who we are and the competition we face?" EBAC's strategy to address this question, posed either way, could be described this way:

> We will become the most responsive organization serving children's mental health needs in our region. Our programs will be created in response to requests from civic leaders, schools, and community groups. We will not compete with the large residential programs, but we will strive to lead the market for school-based services and prevention programs, which are not dependent upon having a large campus and do not require a large investment of capital. Our competitors have enormous overhead on their campuses and, in order to survive, are focused on keeping their residential beds filled. We

---

[24] This story is very well documented and keenly told in Melanie Beene's excellent work, *Autopsy of an Orchestra: An Analysis of Factors Contributing to the Bankruptcy of the Oakland Symphony Orchestra Association* (San Francisco: Melanie Beene & Associates, 1988).

already have a huge head start in the school-based market. We will continually lessen our reliance upon county government funding by diversifying services, securing school district contracts, developing a robust foundation grant income stream for our innovative programs, and growing our individual donor base. We will also begin an endowment for long-term financial flexibility. We will serve kids more effectively in natural community settings, such as schools, and we will make it work financially.

This strategy has worked extremely well for EBAC for nearly three decades. During my tenure it grew from one program serving twenty children to ten programs located at fifteen sites serving more than four thousand children annually. This made EBAC the largest provider, as well as the most responsive one, in the community. Steve Eckart, the current executive director of EBAC, recently confirmed that this positioning continues, with slight modification, to be a key EBAC strategy. In 2007 the organization served approximately nine thousand children.

Most organizational strategies will not be as enduring as these two examples. It is also important to remember that each of these strategies underwent continuous adjustment and that these groups also developed other organizational strategies intended to address other Big Questions.

Let's take a look at a sample of shorter-term organizational strategies that have also served nonprofits well.

California Council for the Humanities (CCH) faced a problem. It offered a range of activities to promote public use of the humanities. However, because it did do so many things at such a small scale it could not have the impact a more focused approach might yield. As CCH's longtime executive director, Dr. Jim Quay, put it: "We are a collection of programs, not an organization." The board and staff decided to change all that. CCH's Big Question was "How can we have the most impact?" They developed a more focused programmatic approach that required a new organizational strategy:

> We will concentrate our financial and staff resources on a single, multi-year statewide initiative, exiting all other programs in a responsible manner. This initiative will give CCH a compelling, focused agenda that will attract both public attention and support

from private and public funders. Since many people do not im-mediately recognize the "humanities," we'll be known as the group that did "that great program."

It took time, fortitude, and a high degree of focus to implement this strat-egy, but in the end CCH did spin off one of its programs into its own sepa-rate organization, transferred another to a more suitable host organization, and closed other activities. It conducted market research and hit on the idea of asking Californians to tell the story of how their family came to the state. The resulting California Stories initiative, launched with a statewide campaign to read *The Grapes of Wrath* during John Steinbeck's centenary in 2002, was an immediate hit with the public, libraries, museums, schools, and donors. The initiative has continued with two other campaigns encour-aging Californians to share their stories with one another. While the choice of the California Stories Project was a programmatic strategy (these will be addressed in Chapter 7), the decision to rebrand the entire organization around it was a profound, and successful, organizational strategy.

The Prescott Circus is a small organization achieving a big impact. It pro-vides circus-based youth-development activities in some of Oakland, Cali-fornia's under-resourced neighborhoods. Prescott is the brainchild of its founder, Aileen Moffit, who has put in countless hours managing every aspect of the operation for many years. She was nearing retirement age and was looking at ways that the organization could continue after her depar-ture. Through a one-day strategy formation session, Moffit and her allies decided that the circus had to continue past her tenure and thus began a process to ensure it would happen. The strategy was quite simple, appro-priate for a small organization without complex systems, but all the more effective for its simplicity:

> We will succeed by providing after-school circus arts instruction augmented by tutoring and support to a growing number of Oak-land schools. We will strengthen our organization before growing to the next stage: develop an advisory committee to raise funds and awareness and create a system for measuring our outcomes. These steps will enhance our ability to attract new, sustainable sources of funding.

Eight times a year music lovers gather in Pittsburgh, Pennsylvania at Synod Hall to hear the best of old music interpreted by the best contemporary performers. The Renaissance & Baroque Society (R&B) has presented more than two hundred concerts of music from the Middle Ages, Renaissance, Baroque, and early Classical periods.

The performance hall where R&B concerts are held is located between the campuses of Carnegie Mellon University, the University of Pittsburgh, and several smaller universities. While R&B has a multitude of potential audience members it could attract to its performances, it has very limited funds available for marketing.

Though it remains a viable presenter at a time when other local arts organizations are struggling for survival, Renaissance & Baroque Society's board and executive director have grave concerns about the future. They know there is limited appeal for the concerts they present and don't expect to expand their audience tremendously. They have had great success raising funds to support an outreach program that sends R&B performers into local schools and medical facilities. They have also been awarded grants from the foundation community to support R&B's programs. As the organization's fortieth anniversary looms on the horizon, R&B is faced with a great challenge and opportunity; it must step up efforts to raise money from individuals.

The Renaissance & Baroque Society's Big Question: "How can we maintain our current programs, plan for bigger projects, and secure the future of the organization?" The organization answered the Big Question with the following organizational strategy:

> To survive, the Renaissance & Baroque Society must continue to offer performances of the highest caliber that will appeal to its subscriber base as well as new audiences. It has maxed its potential unearned revenue from foundations and corporations, so the R&B board must engage much more proactively in individual fundraising.

As R&B plans its fortieth anniversary season, it is the perfect time to implement this strategy. The organization has engaged its audience in a survey to gather input for selecting groups to perform during the season. The board development committee and executive director have established an individual-giving training program for board members, a fundraising goal, and a list of individuals from which to raise those funds. And the executive director has been working with the organization's marketing committee to develop a new logo and merchandise to coincide with the fortieth anniversary season.

Renaissance & Baroque Society's response was multitiered, protecting the core of the organization's mission, while at the same time increasing accessibility and appeal to a wider demographic. The strategy is working—in addition to revenue from ticket and merchandise sales, the organization increased funds raised from individuals by 40 percent, primarily through its special fundraising events and individual solicitations.

As these examples from different nonprofits in different circumstances demonstrate, it is important to constantly monitor both your environment and the effectiveness of your current strategies, and it is essential to respond quickly when a strategy needs adjustment or outright change. Neither of these imperatives is met by the traditional three-year strategic planning cycle. Strategy cannot be relegated to a periodic examination, like an annual physical at the doctor's office. Nor can it be outsourced to consultants. Outside experts can help an organization to structure its thinking, can provide useful tools, and can offer their accumulated professional experience, but, in the final analysis, the organization's strategic health is the board's and management's constant concern.

Conclusion:
Organizational Strategy Comes First

Organizational strategy, from the very tip of the pyramid, is at the heart of successful nonprofit strategic thinking. In this chapter we have reviewed examples of successful organizational strategies and some of the reasons they come into being. Later we will also see that strategy formation is cyclic, although not on a predictable schedule. Next we turn to the question of how organizational strategies such as these are formed.

Chapter Four:
Organizational Identity and Strategy Formation

> **Fail faster, succeed sooner.**
> –David Kelley[25]

THE QUOTE FROM David Kelley, whose IDEO firm has been a top in-novator for two decades, implies that whether you are on the right track or the wrong track, you need to find out before the train gets too far down the line. Indeed, the strategy formation method taught in this book is all about increasing the speed with which your organization learns, adjusts, and then learns some more, quickly adjusting to our rapid-response world. Continually developing and implementing sound strategies is the best way to do this.

So far, this book has shown you the problems with traditional strategic planning, explained what strategy is, and offered some examples of endur-ing, as well as shorter interval, strategies. The next three chapters describe in detail how organizational strategy (the topmost portion of the Strategy Pyramid) can be formed in a more fluid and responsive way than that pro-vided by traditional strategic planning. Before we move on to the critical understanding of the first portion of strategy—organizational identity— let's look at how all the elements of strategy formation combine in a cycle, as illustrated in Exhibit F, Real-Time Strategic Planning Cycle (page 46). As you study the exhibit, note the following progression of steps.

---

[25] David Kelley, CEO, IDEO, as quoted in *Fast Company* (August 1997): 73.

EXHIBIT F Real-Time Strategic Planning Cycle

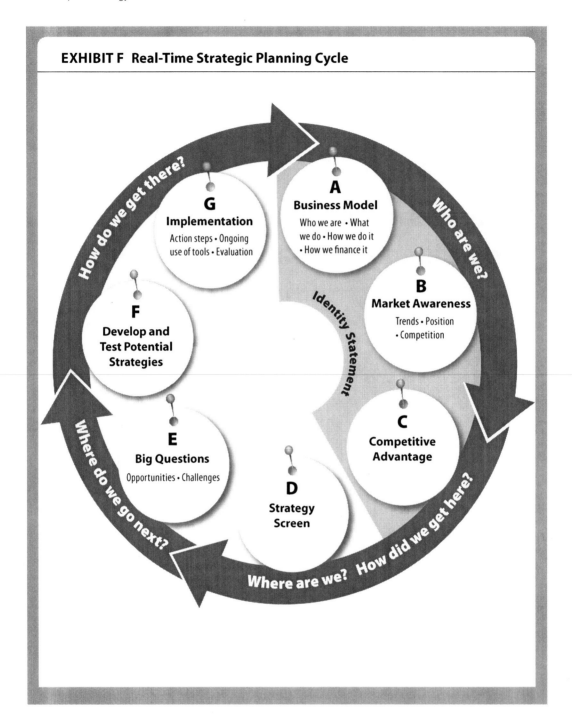

Steps A, B, and **C.** In these steps, you understand who you are as an organization and where you are in the marketplace—your *organizational identity*. This includes three elements: your business model, market awareness, and competitive advantage. (This portion of the Real-Time Strategic Planning Cycle is explained in this chapter.)

Step D. Using your organizational identity, you create a Strategy Screen that helps sort potential strategies. This means you have thought through—before a strategic challenge emerges—the criteria by which you will assess possible strategies that the organization identifies. The screen is an operational expression of your organizational identity. (This is the subject of Chapter 5.)

Step E. Based on your organizational self-knowledge and your understanding of the market, be prepared to recognize and frame a Big Question—a strategic challenge—when it arises. (This is covered in Chapter 6.)

Step F. Develop and test strategies in response to the strategic challenge your organization faces. (This is also covered in Chapter 6; specific programmatic and operational strategies are discussed in Chapters 7 and 8.)

Step G. Implement the strategies and adapt continuously, using the tools in this book and others you have at hand. Through implementation, you will continue to enhance your organization's capacity for each of the other steps in strategy formation. (Tools for developing capacity for strategic thinking and acting are covered on the CD accompanying this book.)

Because the environment you work in is both complex and constantly changing, you cannot expect to form one grand organizational strategy and be done with it for all time. Rather, you must constantly monitor the market you work in to understand where your organization stands—hence the cyclical nature of strategy formation. You must also work to build your organization's operational and strategic capacity to proactively adapt to change as you advance your mission. Dwight D. Eisenhower said of his successful generalship during World War II: "In preparing for battle, I have always found that plans are useless, but planning is indispensable."[26] This effort requires real-time strategic thought and action. Indeed, the ongoing nature of strategy is why we present strategy formation as a continuous cycle rather than a punctuated, time-limited process.

We will revisit strategy formation as a cycle in Chapter 9. Let's move now to the first stage in the cycle—understanding who you are as an organization.

---

[26] Dwight David Eisenhower, as quoted at http://thinkexist.com/quotation/ in_preparing_for_battle_i_have_always_found_that/10642.html.

Understanding Organizational Identity

Organizational strategies are nonroutine. As we saw in the examples from the last chapter, they are needed when you face a significant new Big Question that must be addressed. The Big Question could be an opportunity you may wish to seize or a threat you must counter. The remainder of this chapter will focus on the first three steps in forming an organizational strategy to address a Big Question—clarifying your organizational identity by understanding your business model, your market, and your competitive advantage (Steps A, B, and C in Exhibit F).

The first steps in addressing a particular strategic challenge or Big Question are taken long before that challenge looms. These are noted in the dark gray arrows circling the Real-Time Strategic Planning Cycle in Exhibit F. When undertaking significant strategic work, the organization must know itself (Who are we?), its position in the market (Where are we?), and its history (How did we get here?). Then, when it gets caught up in the complex possibilities inherent in most Big Questions (Where do we go next?) and in finding successful strategies (How do we get there?), it is less likely to lose its way.

We call this core self-knowledge organizational identity. These steps (A, B, and C) sit on top of the light gray background in the center of the Real-Time Strategic Planning Cycle. You should create an organizational identity statement now, so you'll have it when you need it. This fairly simple, although by no means trivial, process provides a sound base upon which to consider your next Big Question. In our experience with the strategy formation project's pilots, and with our own clients, the process of forming the identity statement is itself extremely valuable, and indeed, can be transformative.

There is probably never a time when your organization will lack a Big Question. You cannot stop your current strategic processes while you form an identity statement. Fortunately, it is a process that

---

From Theory to Action:

Real-Time Strategic Planning Kick-Off Session

To develop an organizational identity statement, pull together leaders and other great thinkers in your organization for a single seven-hour meeting, using the process and tools found in the

▶ Facilitator's Guide to Real-Time Strategic Planning (on CD)

is not very time-consuming, and the sooner you get to it the sooner you will start to reap the benefits from this system of thinking. With our project's pilot organizations, and also in our client work, we have found that most nonprofits can develop a clear identity statement during a single seven-hour meeting. (See sidebar, From Theory to Action: Real-Time Strategic Planning Kick-Off Session, page 48). This chapter explains the theory behind the process. However, the process for forming an identity statement is provided in Part 2 of this book, in Tool 6: Identity Statement (page 147).

The development of an organizational identity statement will strengthen all your future strategy work. At the heart of the nonprofit strategy revolution is a focus on deeply knowing your organization, its culture, accomplishments, and internal and external challenges so that you are better prepared to face strategic challenges (your Big Questions) when they arise. Unlike traditional strategic planning's focus on predicting future trends and setting goals to address them, Real-Time Strategic Planning is within your control and is quite doable. It provides you with sound knowledge that can then be used flexibly. You know your organization, but you may never have thought about it in this way before.

Where's the Revolution?

This model presents new ways for you to think about your nonprofit. Rather than seeing it as a collection of programs held together by a board and executive, view it as an entity that applies a business model in a market whose dynamics can be generally understood but usually not controlled. The most revolutionary concept for nonprofits is perhaps that the way to succeed in this market is by *differentiation*: identifying and constantly strengthening a competitive advantage relative to others in the market. Contrast this with traditional strategic planning's focus on goal setting. For most nonprofits, differentiation is revolutionary.

Three Essential Ingredients of Organizational Identity

While a nonprofit will have a single identity statement, it may (in fact it likely will) be working to implement several different organizational strategies at the same time. At the heart of an identity statement, three essentials are required for a nonprofit to have the capacity to form and implement success-

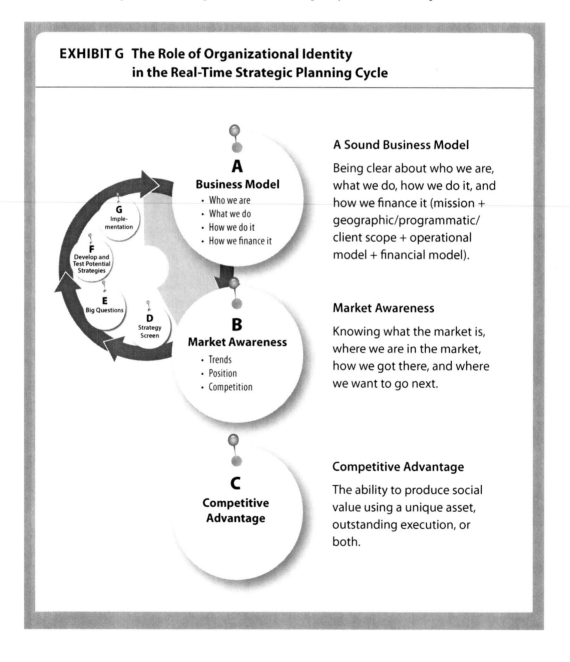

EXHIBIT G   The Role of Organizational Identity in the Real-Time Strategic Planning Cycle

A
Business Model
- Who we are
- What we do
- How we do it
- How we finance it

A Sound Business Model

Being clear about who we are, what we do, how we do it, and how we finance it (mission + geographic/programmatic/ client scope + operational model + financial model).

B
Market Awareness
- Trends
- Position
- Competition

Market Awareness

Knowing what the market is, where we are in the market, how we got there, and where we want to go next.

C
Competitive Advantage

Competitive Advantage

The ability to produce social value using a unique asset, outstanding execution, or both.

G
Imple-
mentation

F
Develop and
Test Potential
Strategies

E
Big Questions

D
Strategy
Screen

ful organizational strategies: a sound business model, market awareness, and competitive advantage. These essentials do not themselves constitute an organizational strategy. Rather, they are the attributes of the organization that enable strategy to be created and successfully implemented—the raw ingredients of organizational strategy. The organization needs to identify these in advance of addressing a strategic challenge (that is, a Big Question).

Let's examine each of these three essentials of organizational identity one at a time.

What is a sound business model?

As a nonprofit you need a business model that outlines

- Who you are—your mission and vision

- What work you do—the activities you undertake to advance your mission and achieve your vision (also called the scope of your work)

- How you do your work—the structure, operations, budgets, policies, and procedures that support your activities, and how you attract and use financial resources

- How you maintain adequate and consistent revenues

> **Sound business model**
>
> Your organization has a *sound business model* when it is clear about:
>
> who it is as an organization
> +
> what work it does
> +
> how it does its work
> +
> how it finances the work

The meaning of the first bullet, *who you are,* is clear—mission and vision are the essence of a nonprofit's identity, and if you are reading this book, you've likely grappled with these issues already. The second bullet, *what work you do,* articulates your scope: where you operate, who you serve, and what you provide. It is also closely related to programmatic strategy as depicted in the Strategy Pyramid (discussed in detail in Chapter 7). What work you do consists of the programs you offer. The third bullet, *how you do your work,* is closely aligned with the concept of operational strategy in the Strategy Pyramid (detailed in Chapter 8).

A sound business model requires that all of these components operate in good form. In addition to a clear and compelling mission and vision, well-conceived and well-executed programs, and sound operations, a nonprofit *must attract sufficient funds and other resources,* the fourth bullet above. If you have each of first three elements, plus a diversified, adequate funding base, then your business model is sound; if not, you need to rethink

From Theory to Action:

Creating Good Mission Statements

If your mission statement is too long, wordy, or filled with semicolons, it needs a trim. A mission statement should be brief and should focus on the ultimate outcomes you are trying to achieve—period. To help you achieve clarity and brevity, see

▶ Tool 20: Mission Statement Refinement (on CD)

it. There is no way around it for a nonprofit (or a business): finances are central to a successful business model.

An inadequate or failing business model is at the center of a great many difficulties that nonprofits experience. An organization may have good programs, but no one willing to pay for them; or perhaps its programs are too expensive to deliver to the target audience. A nonprofit may also have an outmoded program model that is now less appealing than it was a decade ago due to innovations in the field that the nonprofit has not kept up with. Many of our consulting engagements start out with the client posing questions of strategy, branding, funding, or organizational capacity, but the organization's crucial challenge is quickly identified as much bigger than any of these concerns alone: the need for a solid business model. Without this, all else is ultimately futile.

A nonprofit's business model is usually not difficult to identify. A relatively brief, structured conversation among organizational leaders is often sufficient to do so. Nonetheless, such a discussion can lead to startling insights on the part of participants. For example, during a business model discussion:

> An advocacy organization's board member might ask, "If our mission is protecting the rights of immigrants, then why are we involved in a child care initiative? What's the connection?"

> A human services executive director might say, "Our business model just doesn't work. The programs we offer are not bringing in enough money to support themselves. Something has got to change!"

These seemingly straightforward discussions forge links among disparate parts of the organization's life, sometimes for the first time, and can be powerful interventions in themselves. But the real power of these processes comes from putting them together with the next two essentials: market awareness and competitive advantage.

What is market awareness?

Market awareness is a keen and continuously evolving understanding of your current position in the market, field, and sector. It is knowledge of

- What the organization's market is, whether that market is stable, shrinking, or growing, and who else is in the market

- Where the organization stands relative to other players in the market

- How the organization got to its current status relative to others

- Where the organization wants to go next within the market

Market awareness involves seeking answers to a number of questions about the organization's place in the world. This means finding out who else is in the market, their strengths relative to yours, and the state of the market itself—that is, given the current market, is the potential for you (as well as others in your marketplace) to accomplish significant work stable, growing, or shrinking?

Knowing your current situation is just the start, however. You need to understand which of your own and other organizations' actions—as well as which demographic, economic, social, technological, and political forces—have created the current situation. You also need to know what forces may shape your future. With this understanding you can both anticipate future opportunities and address current challenges. This is how organizations succeed for the long term.

If you add a clear understanding and awareness of your market to a sound business model, you will be in a much better position to assess the probable impacts of market trends and factors on your organization. To assess where you are in the effort to achieve your organization's mission and vision, you need to consider what you have learned about your

Market Awareness

Market awareness includes four components. Your organization knows:

what its market is
+
where it is in the market
+
how the organization got to its place in the market
+
where it wants to go next

From Theory to Action:

Conducting Market Research

Part 2 of this book, and the CD that accompanies it, contain tools related to do-it-yourself market research. The following tools will help:

▶ Tool 3: Competitor Analysis (page 131)

▶ Tool 4: Trend Analysis (page 139)

▶ Tool 11: Market Position and Strategy Analysis (on CD)

These processes can dramatically improve your awareness of your place in the market.

business model and your market. The question then becomes: *Given the likely impacts of the market on our business model, how best do we pursue our mission?*

This is the quintessential organizational strategy question. And it is a big one. It is also, obviously, one of the most important and potentially fraught questions you can ask. But considering your competitive advantages can help you find the right answers for your organization. That brings us to our third organizational identity essential.

Where's the Revolution?

Market thinking is fundamentally different from the market analysis used in a traditional three-year nonprofit strategic plan. The market changes quickly, and our ability to predict the future is poor. In the dynamic non-profit environment, developing and honing market awareness is the best way to support good strategic decision making. Rather than analyzing market trends every three years, as occurs for most strategic plans, you must *continually* devote yourself to understanding your current market and your competitors so that you can anticipate changes in time to make adjustments. The best way to do this is to immerse yourself in the process on an ongoing basis.

What is competitive advantage?

The concept of nonprofit competitive advantage, like that of strategy itself, is somewhat different from that commonly used in the business world. We first visited this concept in Chapter 3; now it is time to see how competitive advantage is part of your nonprofit's identity. Here is our definition:

> *Nonprofit competitive advantage* is a nonprofit's ability to sustainably produce social value using a unique *asset,* outstanding *execution,* or both.

Some organizations gain advantage through a unique asset, such as a particular location, a solely owned process or technology, a massive and unbeatable "head start," or even a specific, sought-after individual. But even without such assets, organizations can gain competitive advantage through better execution of programs and management functions than others in their market.

To sustain competitive advantage long term, it is not enough to produce superior outcomes, you also need to know *how* you achieve these outcomes. This means you must dissect your success to determine which programmatic elements are essential, which elements assist, and which are irrelevant or even detrimental. Armed with this understanding, you can better leverage your strengths as well as continually improve your performance—both programmatic and operational—so as not to lose your edge.

Competitive advantage

Your organization's *competitive advantage* is its ability to produce social value using a unique asset, outstanding execution, or both.

Competitive advantage is determined, in part, through comparisons to others: you must provide value, as perceived by clients, members, and other current or potential customers or beneficiaries, not just by your board and staff members.

Your mission represents the social value you strive to create; competitive advantage is the factor that allows you to produce greater social value than the average organization in your market. Thus, competitive advantage differentiates you from others, allowing you to compete effectively for resources such as customers, funds, business opportunities, staff and board talent, and media attention. To be optimally successful in creating social value you must know and consistently employ your competitive advantage.

Our definition of competitive advantage describes two types of advantage—those related to an organization's *assets,* and those related to an organization's *execution.* Let's look at examples of each.

Asset advantages

These involve an inherently better program or other key attribute. For example:

- Better program design leading to better outcomes
- Unique attributes of programs or services, such as linguistic and cultural capacity
- An accessible location, network of locations, or web presence
- A robust, diversified funding base that provides flexibility and stability
- Great name recognition and reputation among funders or members
- Powerful partnerships
- A well-connected board of directors

In the nonprofit sector, as in business, it is very difficult to sustain a substantial asset advantage, if you can even identify one. This is because of the tendency for all new innovations to be quickly and widely adopted. Concepts such as best practices and benchmarking are, essentially, attempts to reduce the disparity between organizations or, put another way, the competitive *dis*advantage caused by asset advantages others have achieved. Here are a few of examples of how this leveling works in the nonprofit sector.

Twenty years ago the treatment of the psychological condition known as depression depended primarily on "talk therapy," which grew out of a psychodynamic understanding of the condition. Results were mixed at best. Then, with the development of effective antidepressant drugs, mental health practitioners began to use a combination of medication and talk therapy. The psychodynamic theory of depression gave way, gradually—and not without a fight—to the current biochemical view. During the transition period, those practitioners (including nonprofit mental health clinics) who were early adopters of drug therapy achieved notably better results than their peers using talk therapy alone. They had found an asset-based competitive advantage! For a short time, forward-looking institutions and practitioners had a market competitive advantage valued by both patients and insurance payers, but then it disappeared. As more effective drugs came on the market, the entire field of depression treatment adopted this approach. The early adopters could still crow that they had been using drug therapy before everyone else caught on, but with time that claim began to ring hollow, as though they were clinging to the successes of the past rather than striving for the next cutting-edge development.

Similarly, when the movement to deinstitutionalize developmentally disabled people began in the 1970s, programs that developed group homes, supervised work activities, and day activity centers had an asset-based competitive advantage over the old-line institutions that had traditionally "warehoused" the disabled. Soon, however, the idea caught on, laws changed, and now community-based living and skill development is the norm. The asset advantage disappeared.

When arts presenters began online ticketing, allowing patrons with Internet access to search for shows, view seating options, and then buy tickets from the comfort of their homes, those with the first effective online functions seized a quite brief competitive advantage. Soon, however, nearly every substantial arts presenter in the country followed suit. It became a serious *dis*advantage to not have an online ticketing capability, but possession of such a system was no longer a differentiating capacity for a few industry leaders.

Or take an example from politics. When Howard Dean sprang onto the scene during the 2004 presidential campaign, perhaps the most notable element of his primary campaign effort was its use of the Internet for grass-roots fundraising. He stood alone in doing this, which gave him both a monetary and an image advantage over his Democratic rivals. Now, candidates from both major parties are using this tool. The competitive advantage of Dean's asset—Internet fundraising—is gone: it is now the norm.

From a societal perspective, the tendency for successful social innovations to be widely copied and broadly embraced is beneficial. It is satisfying to note that we do, in fact, work in a sector where best practices are sought. But from a competitive perspective, this same tendency makes differentiation based on real uniqueness extremely difficult to attain, and once attained, difficult to maintain for long. Thus, it is great if you can develop a true asset advantage—but don't count on it lasting for long. In the world of high technology, strategists assume that each great innovation their company brings to market will be copied immediately and mercilessly, improved, and then priced more cheaply by their competitors. Their only hope is to keep innovating faster than the competition, staying one step ahead of the pack. Nonprofit leaders who believe their asset-based competitive advantage will endure should take heed and focus on continual learning, investment in research and development, and adaptation to remain competitive.

Execution advantages

If you do not have an asset advantage, or if you had one and lost it through the processes just described, don't despair. At most times, in most fields, competitive advantage will be in the form of better execution, not in owning a completely different or better idea, technology, or process. Some examples include

- Lower overall costs to funders or members
- Greater value through efficiency in delivering services per dollar spent
- Faster delivery of services, for example, quickest to respond in a crisis
- Sound marketing and communications that raise visibility and awareness
- Better accountability and public reporting

To return to an example from above, once the entire field adopted community-based living as the more effective and humane approach to helping people with developmental disabilities to function as fully as possible, what then remained to differentiate the better organizations from the rest? The key factor was not *what* they do, since everyone practiced within the same paradigm, but *how* they do it. If, in a given community, 50 percent of developmentally disabled adults receiving assistance from organizations like yours manage to live mostly independently, but your organization can legitimately report a 70 percent success rate, this distinction constitutes a powerful execution-based competitive advantage. Of course, it is possible that superior performance could also be the result of an asset advantage—an inherently better, unique program design—but if so, copycats will close the gap in performance and outcomes will rapidly narrow. Again, while this may be good for society, it can be challenging for your organization.

Where's the Revolution?

The concept of competitive advantage is central to business strategy but largely absent from nonprofit thinking. Breaking the concept down as we have here into asset advantages and execution advantages requires thinking about your organization in what is probably an entirely new way—and one that will not occur during a traditional strategic planning exercise. See *Play to Win: The Nonprofit Guide to Competitive Strategy* for a more in-depth treatment of this key concept.*

* David La Piana with Michaela Hayes, *Play to Win: The Nonprofit Guide to Competitive Strategy* (San Francisco: Jossey-Bass, 2005).

What Organizational Identity Looks Like

You now understand the concept of organizational identity, as well as its three key components—a sound business model, keen market awareness, and competitive advantage. But how do organizations express their organizational identity? Here are some examples of identity statements from pilot groups.

Active Voice (national media organization):

We help people use media for dialogue and social change within the United States. While our work targets the public, our customers are philanthropists and film producers, corporations and movie studios. Our CEO is the recognized field leader and our highly regarded, diverse staff attracts new clients by advancing socially just public policy. We are developing new clients—studios, corporations, and national nonprofits—augmented by foundation grants, building a sustainable revenue mix.

Arc of Hilo (Hawai'i-based human service provider):

We succeed by providing a range of quality services, and being known and trusted by the local community. We serve adults with disabilities in Hilo and other areas of East Hawai'i. Our services include expanded client support, commercial services work opportunities, and residential units. We want to both employ and make employable more individuals with disabilities than any other provider on the island. We will continue to diversify our funding streams, as well as pursue new and sustainable funding through revenue generating business ventures that employ our clients. We strive to become known as the number one provider of disability services on the island of Hawai'i.

And one that was written in a table format:

Renaissance & Baroque Society
(Pittsburgh-based early music presenter):

Components of identity statement	Identity statement
We advance our mission of	fostering a broad understanding of the music, arts, and culture of the Renaissance and Baroque periods in Europe
and seek	broader exposure, to present the best, and to expand and educate our audiences
by serving	individuals and groups, focusing on baby boomers through active retirees
in	Allegheny County—focusing on the East End
through	performance, outreach, education, and events
and emphasizing our competitive advantage of	diverse and quality programming that is not available elsewhere in the region, customer service, and a high-quality web site.

Components of identity statement	Identity statement
We are sustainable by	expanding the audience, corporate underwriting, and tapping more donors in more ways (large donors, bequests, etc.).

Conclusion: **Organization, Know Thyself**

These essentials—the identity statement composed of a sound business model, market awareness, and competitive advantage—form the tools for thinking about organizational strategy, the topmost part of our Strategy Pyramid. Understanding and periodically reviewing these essentials can keep your organization strategically sharp and will likely help it move to a better position in the market than those competitors that rely on a traditional three-year strategic planning cycle. As noted, this entire process, plus the development of a Strategy Screen, can be completed in a one-day kick-off session described in the Facilitator's Guide to Real-Time Strategic Planning (included on the CD accompanying this book). Try it.

Remember that this is a process to undertake *in advance* of a critical need for a new strategy, because it contains the precursors of good strategic thinking. In Chapter 5, you will learn how to put this thinking to use in your organization today, using Strategy Screens—a simple but powerful concept that will drive strategy making within your organization.

Chapter Five:
Developing a Strategy Screen

*There is nothing so useless as doing efficiently
that which should not be done at all.*

—Peter Drucker[27]

PETER DRUCKER'S FAMOUS admonition is one more reminder that we must make the right choices and take the right actions. To do this, we need a sound basis for decision making. This doesn't mean that your organization must identify one all-encompassing strategy that it can pursue for all eternity. Strategy formation, adjustment, and implementation are ongoing processes. Sometimes, as in the case of the Oakland Symphony (which distinguished itself from the far bigger and better-known San Francisco Symphony) or EBAC (which grew to prominence through exploitation of a market niche ignored by competitors), an organization finds an enduring organizational strategy that is quite pervasive in its impact on the organization. At other times strategies are more limited in focus and time frame. The point is that organizations form strategies for many purposes, and usually pursue multiple strategies at once. The Strategy Screen can help.

> A *Strategy Screen* is a set of criteria that your organization uses to choose whether or not a particular strategy is consistent with its identity.

---

[27] Peter Drucker quoted at http://thinkexist.com/quotation/
there_is_nothing_so_useless_as_doing_efficiently/11723.html.

Note that in the Real-Time Strategic Planning Cycle, the Strategy Screen occupies Step D, the fourth circle in the cycle. The Strategy Screen is a transition point between the organization's expression of its identity (Who are we?) and the way in which it seeks its future (Where are we going?). As you will learn in this chapter, the Strategy Screen effectively expresses the organization's identity in a set of selection criteria for choosing future strategies—and hence future direction.

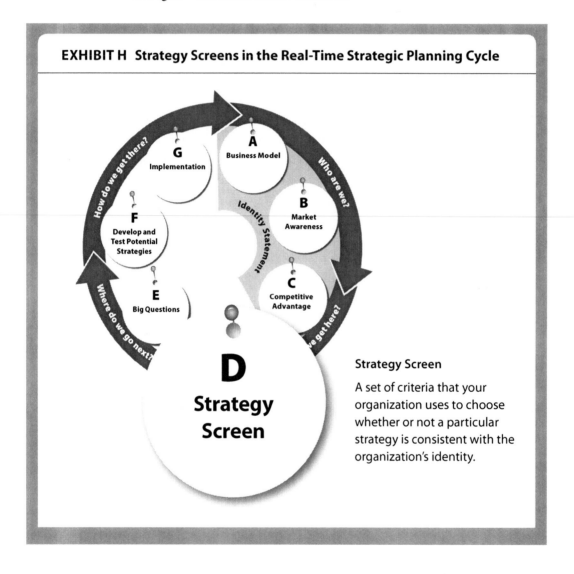

EXHIBIT H   Strategy Screens in the Real-Time Strategic Planning Cycle

Strategy Screen

A set of criteria that your organization uses to choose whether or not a particular strategy is consistent with the organization's identity.

Crafting a Strategy Screen

The Strategy Screen should be developed ahead of time—before a particular Big Question arises and often as part of a Real-Time Strategic Planning kick-off session—so that in the process of responding to a Big Question the organization can focus on picking the best strategy, consistent with its identity. Because Big Questions arise rapidly and often seemingly out of the blue, you may not feel you have the luxury of adequate time to consider your response to a Big Question in the context of your identity statement. The Strategy Screen, conceived carefully rather than in haste, assures that your response to a Big Question is consistent with your organization's mission, direction, and capabilities. Or to paraphrase Peter Drucker, it will help you avoid making a choice to do something efficiently that you shouldn't be doing at all.

The specific criteria you will include in your Strategy Screen depend upon your organization's mission, identity, and competitive advantages, and your assessment of your current market position. The criteria will

- Be different for each organization
- Evolve over time as the organization adapts to changes in the environment
- Usually include five to eight elements

A Strategy Screen is a simple, powerful tool for decision making. It includes the criteria your decisions are based on, and explicitly defines your values. Be sure to develop your Strategy Screen with a group of good strategic thinkers (see Tool 14: Strategic Thinkers Group on the CD) and then vet it widely before adoption. Doing this will serve both to refine the screen and to educate all stakeholders about its importance and use. Strategy Screens are extremely useful when a complex issue emerges and the group is not clear how to proceed. Using a Strategy Screen created before the problem emerged helps focus the discussion and can defuse tensions.

In Exhibit I, Sample Strategy Screen (page 64), the criteria in column one would have been decided in advance of any strategic challenge the organization might face. Once the challenge or Big Question emerges, columns A, B, C, and D would each contain one of the possible specific strategies the organization would consider to address the challenge. The group can simply discuss each option relative to the specific criteria, or may rank the fit as high (3), medium (2), low (1), or no fit (0), tallying the numbers to get a sense of the best choice.

EXHIBIT I Sample Strategy Screen

Options A, B, C, and D are the possible specific strategies an organization is considering. The group can simply discuss each option relative to the specific criteria, or may rank the fit as high (3), medium (2), low (1), or no fit (0), tallying the numbers to get a sense of the best choice.

	Option A	Option B	Option C	Option D
We will undertake strategies that				
1. Are consistent with our mission *				
2. Build on or reinforce our current competitive advantage(s) *				
3. Will break even or produce a surplus within twelve months (or have a source of dedicated funding)				
4. Will yield a result that is sustainable—not fleeting				
5. Will not put us in competition with ABC, because our collaborative relationship with them is essential				
6. Will reinforce the community's view of us as their provider of choice				

* Items 1 and 2 should be in every Strategy Screen. Other criteria are provided as samples; actual criteria will vary from one organization to the next

The criteria in Exhibit I, while hypothetical, represent the range of likely *types* of criteria your Strategy Screen will contain. For example, every organization should insist that any new strategy be consistent with its mission.

Similarly, since a primary aim of strategy is to reinforce your competitive advantages, always include criterion 2 above. The remaining criteria in our example represent value judgments. For example, the organization in Exhibit I has expressed a criterion about sustainability—that any new program will break even or produce a surplus within twelve months (or have a source of dedicated funding). But other organizations might choose to lose money on a particular strategy if they can subsidize the loss in some other way, and if the strategy is otherwise critical to their success. Yet other organizations consistently take on short-term initiatives, so sustainability is not a particular value for them. Again, some organizations are more openly competitive, so would not subscribe to criterion 5.

These criteria are not absolute values. They are organizational choices. Neither is the Strategy Screen, once developed, written in stone. It will develop over time, and may even be violated, consciously, from time to time. For example, the organization in Exhibit I, with a firm rule about sustainability, may encounter an opportunity for a highly valuable program that may never break even. This program may bring greater attention to the organization, helping overall fundraising, or it may fill a gaping need in the community. So the organization decides, in this one case, to violate its rule and take on the program. The important thing is to do this consciously. Everyone should go in with their eyes wide open, knowing that this program will lose money and understanding why that is allowed in this instance. This decision should not set a precedent for other programs—*Hey, we can all lose money!* It is important, therefore, to memorialize this decision at the time so that several years later you can explain to the new board chair why the particular program still loses money each year.

The Strategy Screen is not a rigid framework. Its value is in making your decision-making criteria explicit. Knowing why you are making a specific decision (and being able to articulate your assumptions) is an important strategic capacity because it challenges your thinking, helps you to bring others along in embracing strategic decisions, and creates an organizational memory composed of the rationale for past decisions.

Once you have created a Strategy Screen, you need to share it widely within your nonprofit, solicit feedback, and modify it as circumstances develop over time.

> **From Theory to Action:**
>
> ## Strategy Screen
>
> For a blank version of and instruction sheet for the Strategy Screen, see
>
> ▶ Tool 7: Strategy Screen (on CD)

A Variation—The Opportunity Matrix

Organizations that have been around for some time, or have leaders who like to start new things frequently, develop a great many programs. Others, perhaps by virtue or reputation or specific field, are continually faced with new opportunities. For these organizations, a typical Big Question is "Which opportunity do we pursue?" The Opportunity Matrix is a variation on the Strategy Screen that may be of use in such circumstances.[28] It is a filter for examining the relative value of various strategies, programs, or activities. The Opportunity Matrix helps the organization identify its greatest opportunities and then tighten its focus around those opportunities—in other words, to set priorities.

As with the Strategy Screen, engage a strategic thinkers group where smart people from all parts of your organization come together to develop the Opportunity Matrix. This group should develop four to six key criteria for considering how to tighten the focus of the organization. This process, undertaken seriously, can surface differences in the relative value of different strategies, programs, or activities. It points to the places of greatest opportunity.

Exhibit J, Sample Opportunity Matrix (page 67), shows an organization with five programs (columns A through E), with the opportunity criteria listed at the left. Simply discuss each option relative to the specific criteria, or rank the fit as high (3), medium (2), low (1), or no fit (0), tallying the numbers to get a sense of the best choice.

---

[28] After using the Strategy Screen for some time we developed the Opportunity Matrix. It is presented here both for its own merits (since many organizations face the strategic challenge of too many opportunities) and to encourage you to be creative in how you approach, modify, and use any of the tools we present.

EXHIBIT J Sample Opportunity Matrix

Simply discuss each option relative to the specific criteria or rank the fit as high (3), medium (2), low (1), or no fit (0), tallying the numbers to get a sense of the best choice.

Program / Activity	A	B	C	D	E
	Land acquisition program in Too Tall Hills	Land acquisition program at the lake	Advocacy program	Stewardship program	Education program
What is its value to our mission?	2	3	2	1	3
Economics: Does it pay for itself?	2	2	1	1	3
What's our competition?	3	3	1	2	2
Do we have the capacity?	3	3	1	1	2
Score	10	11	5	5	10

While you will no doubt have other criteria to add, the following should always be part of the Opportunity Matrix.

Value. This is the relative importance of an activity to the mission. The group should rate it (3) high, (2) medium or (1) low. Push yourselves to differentiate between various activities—do not simply label them all as high value—that says nothing.

Economics. This is a description of the economic logic of the activity, program, or strategy. Consider whether the opportunity has a dedicated income stream, generates a surplus or a deficit, or has potential for improving its economic logic. Think prospectively and use a spreadsheet so these determinations are based on real numbers. For example, eliminating a program that has a dedicated but inadequate funding stream (such as a government contract that pays 90 percent of your related program costs) may only make the financial loss worse. Instead of losing a few thousand dollars a year while providing a useful service, by giving up the contract the organization loses the program's contribution to its overhead, which may be substantial. Rate it (3) strong, (2) medium, or (1) weak.

Competitiveness. There are two considerations here. First, is this activity or strategy undertaken in a highly competitive market, making for difficult work? Is your organization the market leader, one of many, or a small fry? Second, if there are no other organizations in this market (because it is a money-losing proposition), is there an overriding value concern that keeps your organization there? For example, the last hospital in a rural area has no competitors, and regularly hemorrhages dollars, but if closing it would leave the community without health care, that may be an overriding concern. The group may decide to keep the hospital going for as long as possible. You can rate each activity (3) strong, (2) medium, or (1) weak relative to its competitive position.

Organizational Capacity. Essentially, the question is "How easy is it for us to produce this activity?" Does it require specialized skills, equipment, or expensive outside specialists, or is it a routine activity that the organization inherently understands how to produce? Also, consider whether the activity or program places heavy or relatively light demands on the organization's administrative capacities. Rate each activity or program (3) high, (2) medium, or (1) low in terms of your capacity to deliver it.

These four elements encapsulate the criteria most nonprofits should consider when facing difficult but necessary focusing decisions. However, feel free to add other criteria if they better suit your needs. Using these criteria, you can quickly gauge the relative strength of any actual or proposed activity. This will help you make decisions based on apples-to-apples comparisons between options.

In our example, a fictional land trust, we see that the organization has two very high value programs: its land acquisition work (expressed in two programs) and its education program based in the local schools. Its stewardship program (managing land until it is disposed of to a public body) is not a very highly valued activity. As you can see, it is more of a necessary evil. Advocacy, which the organization believes is fairly important, is a losing proposition from a financial perspective. The land trust is not very adept at it and has little in the way of funds to invest in it. Between its two land acquisition programs, one is more highly valued, but both are strong activities—no surprise, as this is the core of what the organization does. We learn from this exercise that education, a noncore activity for a land trust, is actually very important and perhaps deserving of more attention, while advocacy is perhaps best left to another organization adept at this specialized work.

> From Theory to Action:
>
> **Opportunity Matrix**
>
> For a sample blank version and instructions for using the Opportunity Matrix, see
>
> ▶ Tool 23: Opportunity Matrix (on CD)

Whatever criteria you use, develop your Opportunity Matrix as a group process, with other organizational leaders. Argue over it; vet every entry. Do not allow yourself or others to be deluded about the facts around a pet program. When—and only when—you have completed and agreed upon the elements of an Opportunity Matrix, you can discuss it and begin to make decisions about prioritization, either for growth or for cutting back, depending upon your circumstances.

Conclusion: **Habits of Mind**

The Strategy Screen and the Opportunity Matrix variant are simple, powerful tools that help decision makers become more strategic. They are also habits of mind. That is, the first time you try to use one of these tools it may feel somewhat artificial or forced, but as you have more experience with the process, it becomes a familiar discipline for decision making. Remember, this is not a one-time activity. Use these tools whenever a question arises that they might help you to better understand. Every nonprofit should have an updated Strategy Screen for use in selecting organizational strategies. The Opportunity Matrix is most helpful when you are comparing different programs, either current or potential, for overall value to the mission and organization.

With a clear sense of organizational identity, and with the few simple tools we have provided thus far, you are ready to tackle the concept of the Big Question itself.

Chapter Six:
Big Questions, Strategy Formation, and Implementation

> There is always a better strategy than the one you have;
> you just haven't thought of it yet.
>
> —Sir Brian Pitman[29]

THIS CHAPTER PRESENTS the concept of Big Questions and explores how to address them, using the Strategy Screen process. It is wise to keep in mind, as Sir Brian reminds us, that every strategy, no matter how successful or beloved, is probably in some way not quite optimal. It is just the nature of organizational life—perfection is never within reach. Moreover, a new opportunity or challenge can arrive at any time, rendering our beloved way of doing things suboptimal, or even downright useless. Thus, we should always be open to developing new strategies—and not just when our current strategies are in trouble.

Understanding and Facing Big Questions

Let's take a moment to define the term Big Question. A central tenet of the nonprofit strategy revolution is that good strategic thinking is most critical when the organization must decide whether and how to respond to a potentially significant opportunity or challenge. Though I have used the

---

[29] Sir Brian Pitman, former CEO, Lloyds TSB, as quoted at www.12manage.com/quotes_s.html.

term Big Question throughout this book, now is the time for a definition, however informal.

> A *Big Question* is an opportunity or threat to which the organization must respond. Usually, it is beyond the scope of the organization's current strategies, thus requiring a new strategy.

A Big Question typically comes in one of three forms. It may offer an opportunity to do something new, or to take a thing currently done to a

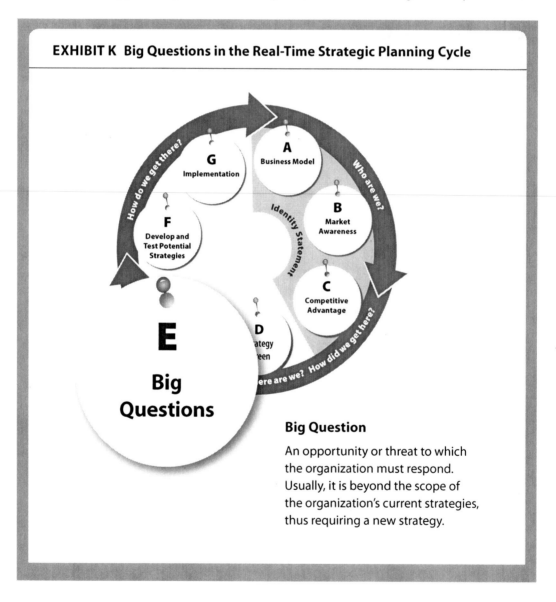

EXHIBIT K Big Questions in the Real-Time Strategic Planning Cycle

Big Question

An opportunity or threat to which the organization must respond. Usually, it is beyond the scope of the organization's current strategies, thus requiring a new strategy.

greater scale. It may be a threat or barrier to what you are doing now, with a negative impact on your organization. Or it may challenge your business model itself. These categories are shown in Exhibit L (page 75), under "3. Big Question." Let's look at each of these three possibilities in turn.

New Opportunity. A new strategic opportunity is present when the organization perceives that, with effort, timing, and luck, it can measurably improve its ability to advance its mission through widening the scope of its activities. The opportunity might be a funder's request for proposals that could increase program size, a sorely needed new building in a choice location that has come on the market for sale, or a strategic restructuring possibility with an attractive partner. New opportunities are usually exciting and, at first blush, may also seem daunting. "How could we take advantage of that," the organization asks itself, "when we are so busy with our current activities?" The Big Question becomes "Should we do this and, if so, how?" An earlier example of a New Opportunity Big Question was that faced by Ruth Bolan, former director of O'hia Productions, when her children's theater company encountered two wonderful opportunities that challenged its capacity (see Chapter 1, page 17).

Competitive Challenge. A competitive challenge is present when another organization, whether for-profit, nonprofit, or governmental, is acting in ways that can (often unintentionally) harm your organization. It might be a rival theater that builds a new state-of-the-art facility in town, a health care corporation that decides to compete with your community health clinic, or a fellow advocacy organization (with whom you may agree on matters of substance) that is siphoning off media attention and members from your group. Competitive challenges are usually frustrating and a bit scary. "How dare they!" is often the organization's first reaction. The Big Question becomes "What can we do about this to preserve or strengthen our market position?"

Business Model Challenge. A challenge to your business model is similar to a competitive challenge, except in this regard: it is a challenge to both your organization and all of your competitors who have similar program designs. For example, when governmental rate-setting authorities consistently keep payment levels to group homes for troubled kids so low that organizations cannot meet the staffing and other requirements those same governmental agencies mandate (the situation for many years in some states), *all* group home providers are in trouble. Similarly, when the Internet makes it unnecessary for anyone with online access to visit a bricks-and-mortar volunteer center for help finding a volunteer opportunity, a life-or-death business model challenge faces all volunteer centers. If the potential volunteer can find a place to volunteer on the Internet, there is no need for the intermediary role of the volunteer centers.[30]

Business model challenges (such as that faced by volunteer centers) tend to "sneak up" on an industry. What at first seems an irrelevancy soon becomes a concern and then, before we know it, a full-blown threat. Meanwhile, the best, and often the only effective, response to such a challenge requires all current competitors to work together, something they may not be accustomed to doing. The Big Question here might be "Can our current business model survive this new threat?"

When one of these three types of Big Questions is present, you need a process for addressing it. Here is how it works.

Crafting a Big Question

If you have been following the Real-Time Strategic Planning process as I have presented it, you have developed an identity statement. Along the way, you have gained a good understanding of your business model, market position, and competitive advantage. You have also created a Strategy Screen and perhaps an Opportunity Matrix. Thus, your staff and organization have prepared, in a more relaxed and unpressured time, for the crucible of the next Big Question.

Now comes the moment of truth—a new Big Question is on the horizon. Or perhaps, more accurately, it has just landed with a loud *thunk* on your desk. You need an organizational strategy to respond to it—not in six months or a year, but soon, in real time.

Exhibit L, Strategy Development, provides a decision tree for thinking about how to respond to a Big Question. As you can see, it is also possible to decide *not* to respond.

---

[30] This threat is referred to as "disintermediation."

EXHIBIT L Strategy Development

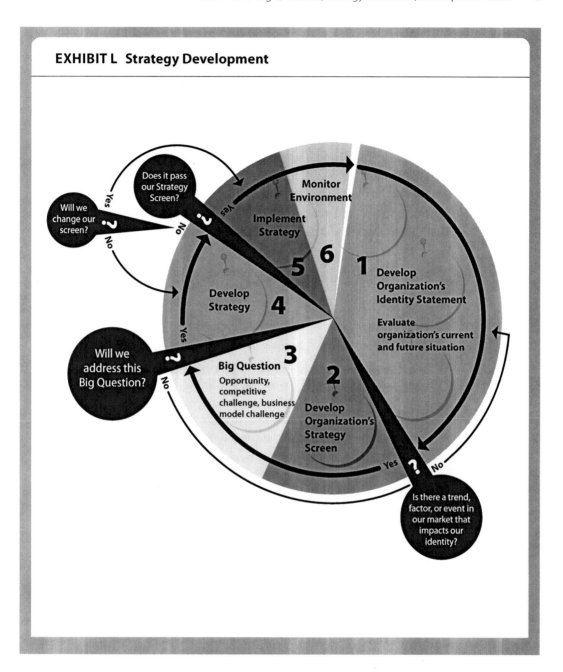

To successfully address a Big Question, you first have to know what the right question is to ask. Sound simple? It's not. A Big Question is a strategic challenge, and as such it must be understood in terms of the organization's mission, context, and priorities. For example: Let's say your state legislature decides to eliminate its funding for local arts councils, which have been a big source of money and of a sense of community among small arts presenters and individual artists all over the state. (This actually happened in California a few years ago.) You are the executive director of an arts group that has been very involved with your local arts council, receiving significant funding from it over many years. You understand immediately that this move by the state presents a Big Question. But what, exactly, is the question? Is it

A. How can we replace the funding we'll lose when the arts council closes?

B. How can we balance the budget with less money?

C. How will the loss of the arts council impact organizations like ours across the state, and therefore, how will we respond as a community?

D. What does this mean about the future of the arts in our communities? Will there be more cuts? Will this cut be restored next session?

Each of these formulations asks the question differently, emphasizing a different part of the problem the state's move creates. In every case, however, it can be understood as a business model challenge, since the problem is not caused by a competitor and it is experienced by nearly every arts organization in the state.

Option A presents the simplest and starkest dilemma: We have some money, we depend on it, we are going to lose it, so what should we do to replace it?

Where's the Revolution?

Traditional strategic planning tends to focus on future-oriented goals that are often only tenuously tied to current challenges, in spite of everyone's best efforts. The Big Question offers an opportunity to bring strategic thinking to bear on well-articulated current challenges or opportunities. The resulting work will not sit on a shelf gathering dust but rather will constitute an organizational call to action in response to the identified challenge or opportunity.

"Ms. Jones, there are a number of big questions here to see you. They say they won't leave until they have some answers."

If this is the Big Question you ask, then possible strategies could involve increased fundraising from other sources or perhaps consideration of a social enterprise to generate cash.

Option B asks the reverse of Option A. Instead of focusing on revenue replacement, asking the question in this way would likely lead to budget cutting and staff layoffs.

Option C frames the Big Question as a business model challenge: the entire arts community is affected, calling for a combined response. Likely strategies to emerge from this framing of the question include coalition building and advocacy.

Option D similarly defines the Big Question as a business model challenge, focusing on the near-term future. If we believe the cuts will be restored next year, then we'll just find a way to hang on, but if we think there may be even deeper funding cuts in the future we may have to change our business model to adjust to the new reality. Likely strategies involve coalition building and advocacy, but also political research and an attempt to gauge the legislative climate so that operational changes are made accordingly.

None of these articulations is inherently right or wrong. In fact, one could envision several more. However, the question you ask will to a large degree determine the strategies you form. For example, note that the way options A and B are framed suggests fundraising or cutback strategies (essentially they are opposite sides of one another), while Option C suggests coalition building, and Option D suggests hanging tight.

It is wise to articulate the Big Question in many different ways and then characterize each as I have done so that you can see the choices each different framing offers. In the end you may decide that the Big Question needs to be addressed on several, or even all of these dimensions, and so you combine the different framing options into one. For example,

> How can we respond to the loss of the arts council's funding? Can we replace it from other sources, or will we need to cut expenses? How will the loss of the arts council impact organizations like ours across the state? Is this a temporary setback or the beginning of a trend of more cuts?

Let's label this one Option E. It provides a fuller picture of the ramifications of this move by the state. It also complicates the answer, as different emphases may lead to conflicting strategies, which is all to the good. The process of formulating the question in this way will lead to a more subtle, complex, and hopefully successful strategic answer. If I were the executive director of this organization, given the information at hand, I would choose Option E as giving me the greatest chance of "getting it right" in the end.

Developing a Strategy That Fits the Screen

Using the Strategy Screen you have previously created, you can assess potential strategies as you develop them. Continuing with the arts council example, let's assume you define the question in its most complex form, Option E:

> How can we respond to the loss of the arts council's funding? Can we replace it from other sources, or will we need to cut expenses? How will the loss of the arts council impact organizations like ours across the state? Is this a temporary setback or the beginning of a trend of more cuts?

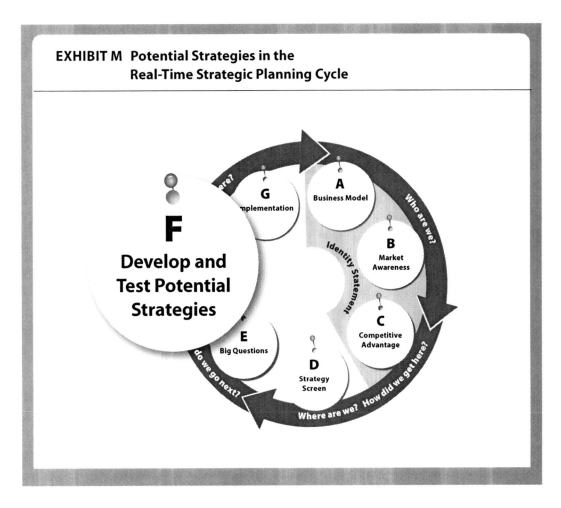

EXHIBIT M Potential Strategies in the Real-Time Strategic Planning Cycle

As you formulate possible responses, you might categorize them as follows.

1. *Greater independence.* This budget cut provides a wake-up call. We need to become less dependent on the capriciousness of the state government. This has happened before, and even if the legislature replaces the funding this time there is too much instability in our reliance upon the state's whims. We need to develop more diversified funding. We will do this by reviewing our ticket pricing policies, looking into the possibility of selling more and higher profit merchandise at our theater store, and focusing our board's attention on major giving. At the same time, we need to review every line item and see where we can squeeze costs out of the budget without doing harm.

2. *Political action.* We need to fight this at the political level through our coalition of arts organizations across the state. We have members in every legislative district and need to make them feel our presence. We believe we can reverse these cuts next year, and will make doing so our top priority. In the meantime, we will make an extraordinary appeal to our donors for one-time funds in the crisis, and if necessary we will dip into our reserve funds. There is no room to cut our current budget without doing harm, so this will be a last resort.

As you can see, these potential strategies take quite different approaches to answering the Big Question. Each fits our basic definition of a strategy as *an organized pattern of behavior toward an end.* Each consists of several linked behaviors—actions the organization will take—that intend to accomplish the same end. In the first proposed strategy, the organization decides to move away from reliance on an unpredictable public source of funds through a series of related actions involving both revenue growth and cost cutting. In the second proposed strategy, the organization decides to fight the budget cuts using political action. Confident of success, it is unwilling to make drastic cost reductions that will do long-term harm to the organization, and instead proposes to rely on short-term and one-time fixes while it fights a battle it hopes to win.

Note that each of these proposed strategies is just that: a strategy, not a goal. The difference is that strategies entail patterns of behavior—interlinked actions—rather than specific outcomes. These strategies will lead to the development of goals such as "increase fundraising revenue by 10 percent over two years," or "raise ticket prices by an average of $2 next year." But those goals are in the service of carrying out the larger strategies, a step that is often missing in traditional strategic plans.

Exhibit N, Sample Strategy Screen for Theater (page 81), demonstrates how these proposed strategies might stack up using a fictional, but reasonable, Strategy Screen.

Reviewing the proposed strategies in this way, the organization has articulated a clear choice of directions in responding to this Big Question. While every choice is fraught with risk, and will require an investment of time and money, doing nothing could well be the most dangerous path of all. Assuming you have already developed a Strategy Screen, the articulation of the Big Question and vetting of different strategies can be accomplished relatively quickly, allowing you to focus your efforts next on implementation.

EXHIBIT N Sample Strategy Screen for Theater

	Option A Greater Independence	Option B Political Action
We will undertake strategies that		
1. Are consistent with our mission	Yes, we will be stronger with more diverse funding	Yes, we need to keep the state funding
2. Build on or reinforce our current competitive advantage (*Our competitive advantage is presenting new dramas not available elsewhere in our city*)	Yes, selling selected, high-quality, show-related merchandise may strengthen our brand recognition	This strategy neither builds on nor detracts from our competitive advantage
3. Will break even or produce a surplus within twelve months (or have a source of dedicated funding)	Yes, this will lead to replacing lost state funds and will enhance our financial strength	If we restore the cuts we'll be back where we are today. But unless our one-time appeal brings in enough money, we will need to spend a portion of our surplus
4. Will likely yield a result that is sustainable—not a flash in the pan	Yes, this will yield a more diverse and sustainable income mix	If we succeed—the state, despite its problems, has been a good source of ongoing funds for a long time
5. Will not put us in competition with ABC, because our collaborative relationship with them is essential	Since we are not changing our work there will be no change in our relationship	This strategy will require us to work even more closely with ABC, and with all others across the state
6. Will reinforce the community's view of us as their theater of choice (*Our positioning and competitive advantage again*)	Yes, the merchandising element will aid with this. We must be careful not to price our tickets too high—we want the younger demographic	No impact—or could be a positive impact if the community sees us as "fighting city hall"

Testing strategies

Testing strategies is an important step prior to selection, but it need not be too time-consuming if you use a commonsense rather than a formal research-oriented approach. Indeed the time invested in determining whether a strategy is feasible is usually very well spent—especially if the selected strategy turns out to not be feasible.

There are a few basic approaches to testing strategies.

The Reality Check. Is this proposed strategy at all feasible? What will it cost in money, needed media attention, or person hours, either from staff or volunteers? Is it reasonable to build a strategy that requires these levels of investment? You can try to answer these questions by asking the right people—perhaps your board chair, your finance person, and others who have both a clear eye for the facts and less investment in this particular strategy than the people who created it.

The Laugh Test. If you describe your proposed strategy to colleagues, funders, and other thoughtful advisors, can they see you and your organization pulling it off? In the example of the theater above, if the proposed strategy were to "take our most successful stage productions on the road around the country, like a Broadway touring company, thus making lots of money," it might be wise to run it by an advisor who knows both your organization and the theater business. Or if your strategy involves relying on the goodwill of the public for political support, but your advisors tell you that your recent negative press coverage has weakened that support considerably, that again is important to know.

The Validity Test. It may be that your proposed strategy fits with your organization's culture and capabilities, and is otherwise entirely feasible, but that even if it is successfully implemented it will not address the Big Question because, simply put, it is not the right strategy. For example, if the theater were to implement a strategy of increased revenues through merchandising, and that could reasonably be expected to yield 5 percent of the organization's total revenues after a couple of start-up years, but the budget crisis was more on the order of 25 percent of those revenues, then investing lots of energy in that strategy might not be wise—unless it were linked to other strategies that could develop the rest of the needed revenues. Sound financial review, perhaps by disinterested and very knowledgeable outsiders, is a good way to test the validity of proposed strategies.

Implementing the Strategy

Once the organization chooses a strategy, it is time to implement it. Let's suppose the arts presenter in our example chooses Option A, "Greater independence." The staff lists a series of linked actions the organization must now take. These include:

1. We need to review our ticket pricing policies, including a comparison with our closest competitors, to see if there is room to raise our prices. We also want to be sure we do not raise them so high that most people in town cannot afford them. We can explore the possibility of tiered pricing or premium seating, where the cost of the best seats increases more than the cost of the rest of the seats.

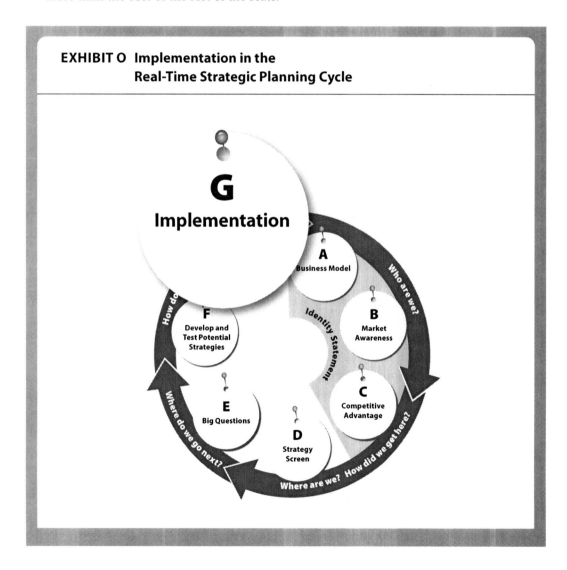

EXHIBIT O   Implementation in the Real-Time Strategic Planning Cycle

2. We must explore the possibility of selling more and higher-profit merchandise at our theater store. In fact, the store could be much more profitable if we remodeled and enlarged it and added more show-specific merchandise. We need also to explore the feasibility of an online store, which will appeal to our younger audience members.

3. We have to talk with the board about a serious ramp-up in their own giving and that of our current and potential major donors. We have lots of small donors, but there are probably people out there who can and would give more if we approached them in the right way.

4. We must review every line item in our operating budget to see where we can squeeze costs out of the budget without doing harm to the quality of our shows or the audience's experience.

In traditional strategic planning these and other possibilities would be explored as part of the overall planning process—that is, if one of these actions happened to be underway at the time the cut was announced. Meanwhile, the organization would be exposed to the full impact of the cuts. Then, months later, someone would be tasked with implementing the actions selected through the planning process. Real-Time Strategic Planning—the process described here—moves the organization to implementation much faster. Take, for example, the budget review (item 4, above). As soon as non-essential costs are uncovered, the process of eliminating them can begin. The authorization for doing so is contained in the strategy the organization has adopted. Management can move in a timely manner from assessing the possibilities in each area to acting on what it finds. This is what we mean by rapid response.

Similarly, each of the other elements of the strategy can proceed directly to implementation, unless the element is found to be infeasible. For example, if competitive and other forces prohibit the organization from raising its ticket prices, the leadership knows immediately that it has one less action available to implement its revenue diversification strategy. This puts added pressure on the remaining actions. If it turns out that none of the actions is feasible, then the organization will need to revisit its selected strategy.

If you have spent the time up front articulating your business model, developing a keen sense of your market position, and understanding your competitive advantages, the chances that you will choose an unworkable strategy are low, because such strategies will be screened out earlier in your consideration. Even if you do eliminate all of your proposed strategies, the elapsed time before you decide you need to develop a different strategy is still far less than that entailed in traditional strategic planning.

This capacity to rapidly discard failed strategies and adopt new ones is a major advantage of the nonprofit strategy revolution. We do not have all the answers and often must act on incomplete information. In this uncertain world, the strategy revolution provides a more flexible, faster, iterative strategy formation process than that offered by traditional strategic planning.

From Theory to Action:

Implementing the Strategy

Execution is everything! Real-Time Strategic Planning will be useless if you do not use it to develop and implement strategy. We offer some good tools to assist in your efforts:

▸ Tool 9: Next Steps Work Plan (page 155)

▸ Tool 10: Strategy Road Map (page 159)

▸ Tool 25: 90-Day Plan for Incremental Improvements (on CD)

Conclusion: **Real-Time Strategy**

This chapter provided a different way of identifying and addressing strategic challenges, one that is available to you when needed rather than on a predetermined three-year cycle, and that is quite flexible in its use. Try it next time you confront a Big Question.

So far, we have been dealing with organizational strategy, the topmost part of the Strategy Pyramid. This is the level where the most difficult organizational choices often occur. But significant programmatic choices also confront the nonprofit leader, and the next chapter addresses these.

Chapter Seven:
Forming Programmatic Strategies

> However beautiful the strategy,
> you should occasionally look at the results.
>
> —Winston Churchill[31]

NOW IT IS TIME to move from organizational strategy, at the top of the Strategy Pyramid, to the center section: programmatic strategy. As Churchill's quip reminds us, no nonprofit's organizational strategy is sound if it results in a suite of programmatic offerings that are ineffective, redundant, or low quality. In a nonprofit, program is where the mission gets carried out.

PROGRAMMATIC
Decide on approaches and offer programs and activities to achieve specific outcomes related to the target audiences

Every nonprofit offers one or more programs or sets of activities: these are the reasons for its existence and constitute its public face. In most fields of nonprofit endeavor there are usually many choices for both what programs to offer and how to deliver them. These choices are determined by your organization's mission; by the desires of your board, staff, and funders; and by your culture and available resources. The questions often break down as follows:

- What programmatic activities should we offer, and at what scale, to most effectively pursue our mission within our resource constraints?

- Where should our programmatic activities be located or delivered?

---

[31] Winston Churchill, as quoted at http://thinkexist.com/quotation/ however_beautiful_the_strategy-you_should/220337.html.

- Who, specifically, within the full range of our target market, should each of our programmatic activities target?

- Based on what we know about our field, including recent developments, what programmatic approaches are most likely to maximize our intended social impact?

- What are we mandated to do, and what are we prohibited from doing, either by law, charter, or by the requirements of any external organizations, including funders, national organizations we are franchised from or divisions of, or accreditation bodies?

Let's take a case example. The Hawai'i Community Foundation (HCF) realized that the biggest barrier to its nonprofit grantees' success was consistent, good leadership. Two studies, *Daring to Lead: Nonprofit Executive Directors and Their Work Experience,* and *Leadership Lost: A Study on Executive Director Tenure and Experience,* provided data to back up the foundation's own experience.[32]

Once HCF recognized that turnover among the state's executive directors was quite high, and that incumbent nonprofit executives lacked access to educational and professional development opportunities that might both increase their skill level and extend their tenure, HCF decided that executive development had to be a major goal for the foundation. But how to get there? It developed a programmatic strategy that featured three parts:

Where's the Revolution?

Traditional strategic planning rarely asks a nonprofit to recognize that its choice of programmatic approach is neither a given nor, once chosen, set forever in stone. Expressing programmatic choices as *strategies,* rather than merely as *the work of the organization,* elevates them to a higher level of scrutiny.

---

[32] Jeanne Peters and Timothy Wolfred, with Mike Allison, Christina Chan, Jan Masaoka, and Genevieve Llamas, *Daring to Lead: Nonprofit Executive Directors and Their Work Experience* (San Francisco: CompassPoint, 2001); Timothy Wolfred, with Mike Allison and Jan Masaoka, *Leadership Lost: A Study on Executive Director Tenure and Experience* (San Francisco: CompassPoint, 1999).

grantmaking for executive development, an annual conference, and a leadership training program.

> Our executive director development strategy will consist of several interlinked approaches. We'll make grants for organizational capacity building projects that support executive development and learning while helping their organizations to address a real problem; we'll sponsor an annual statewide conference for board members, recognizing that executives' success is often limited by their boards' knowledge and motivation; and we'll create a year-long leadership development program for a dozen or so leaders per year so that over time we will develop a cadre of experienced, skilled, and interconnected nonprofit leaders.

Like an organizational strategy, a programmatic one such as this describes a set of intended actions that are linked. (Remember our definition of strategy as an organized pattern of behaviors.) The crucial difference here is that the actions are focused on programmatic choices. Programmatic strategy helps to define what an organization is in the world, but only indirectly. Its direct focus is on finding the best ways to carry out the mission.

Forming Programmatic Strategies

In recent years much has been made of the logic model as a tool for thinking about program design. Some have even advocated logic model development as a substitute for strategic planning. Personally, I believe this tool can be very helpful at the programmatic strategy level, but is too linear for the wide-ranging and often nonlinear concerns of organizational strategy. One good way to produce a programmatic strategy is to employ a logic model approach. The structure, which can be frustratingly linear, forces you to think through the expectations you have for your particular strategy. As you will see, this is a useful discipline.

Constructing a Program Logic Model

A programmatic logic model works like this:

Articulate the *assumptions* upon which you are building your program. Assumptions are your beliefs about how things work, related to your program. For example, "Children who have supportive adults in their lives will do better in school."

Enumerate *activities* you will undertake. Activities are, quite simply, things you will do. For example, "Provide one hundred at-risk five- to ten-year-olds with mentoring from a caring adult."

Anticipate the *resources* required for these activities, both people and money. For example, "The program will require 100 adult volunteers, 3 full-time social workers, and $500,000 a year in funding."

Specify the *outputs* you anticipate from these activities. Outputs are the measurable units of the program's production. For example, "Provide 100 weekly contacts between adults and children in the program, over 40 weeks, equaling 4,000 mentor-child contacts per year."

Describe the *short-term outcomes* that will result from these outputs. Short-term outcomes are positive results of the program that are likely to occur within twelve months. For example, "Children who participate in the program will do better in school, as reported by their parents and teachers."

Finally, imagine the long-term outcomes, often called the *impact*, of the program. These are positive results that can take years to manifest themselves. For example, "At-risk children receiving mentoring will attend college in greater numbers."

Use the programmatic logic model as a tool to help check out your thinking. First of all, testing your assumptions is critical. Often we are not even aware of our assumptions because they are so deeply held. But remember the adage, "When you assume, you make an *ass* of *u* and *me*." Be explicit about what you think are the causes of the problem your program will address, and the likely remedies. Discuss these assumptions widely both inside and outside your organization. If your assumptions are faulty, your whole program design could be flawed, dooming you to failure from the outset.

Similarly, when stipulating what you will actually do to impact a social problem, be aware that these activities need to stand up to close scrutiny. After all, this is where you will spend your time and money carrying out your program. What resources will it take to conduct these activities? What volume or other observable measures (outputs) of these activities do you anticipate? If, for example, you assume that global warming can be stopped by moving people out of their internal combustion cars, but your resources and activities only allow you to reach one city for your advocacy effort, you need to think about the scale of that effort relative to the size of the problem. Perhaps you can network with similar programs in other cities, or states, or even countries, but you *must* recognize that the problem will not be significantly impacted by your activities alone. This is not to say your activities are not worth undertaking; it just requires that you be objective about their scale and the outputs you can achieve with the resources you have. Perhaps rather than "measurably reducing global warming pollutants released into the atmosphere," your output should be "developing a successful model for others to emulate and build upon." Thinking in this way will have a profound impact on your program design. In the example above, the program will need a strong evaluation and dissemination component if it is to serve primarily as an experiment whose results you want others to copy.

> **From Theory to Action:**
>
> ## Logic Models and Value Creation Cycle
>
> The use of a logic model can help you produce and refine a program strategy. An alternative to the logic model is our Value Creation Cycle tool. This tool is less linear than the logic model, and may better represent your situation. The Value Creation Cycle focuses more on the non-profit's current situation and its impact in the short term. Review both the logic model and the Value Creation Cycle, and then decide which is the best tool for your job. For help, see
>
> ▸ Tool 19: Value Creation Cycle (on CD)
>
> ▸ Tool 24: Logic Model (on CD)

Next come the hardest questions. I sometimes refer to these as the "So what?" questions. Let's say you develop and deliver activities based upon your assumptions, using the appropriate resources and at a known scale. For example, "We believe [assumption] that quality child care will enable low-income preschoolers to succeed in kindergarten. We will provide twenty children with this service [activity] daily for the next year [output]." Given the assumption, activity, and output, the question that must be asked is "Did these children go on to succeed in school at higher rates than other kids who did not participate?" Given the complexity of social phenomena, you may not be able to determine the ultimate answer, the *impact* your program achieved, at least not in the near term and not at a reasonable cost. Still, it would not be wise to continue to provide the same service for thirteen years, waiting to see whether your first class of preschoolers graduates from high school, before making adjustments.

For this reason the logic model has *short-term outcomes,* which enable us to project into the future a bit better. For example, it is known that children who learn to read by the third grade do better in school than those who do not. To assess this outcome from the point of preschool you must still wait four years, which is better than thirteen years, but still too long to wait before making adjustments. We also know that children whose parents read to them early in life do better in school. Does the child care program have a component that encourages this behavior from parents? If so, then perhaps this is a short-term outcome that can be measured in months rather than years. There can, of course, be multiple short-term outcomes.

The point here is that social phenomena are so notoriously difficult to measure that we sometimes need proxies—other, more easily observable

EXHIBIT P Programmatic Logic Model

Assumptions	Activities	Resources
Poor children who receive enrichment early in life do better in school	Daily preschool for 20 four-year-olds, 8 a.m.–5 p.m., year round	An inspiring director and 3 teachers $500,000 a year
Parents can help their children's school readiness	Parent education classes for 20 families, 20 weeks a year	A child care licensable building and funds to renovate it
Parents will send their kids to preschool if it is affordable and accessible	Raise sufficient funds to make the program affordable and locate it in the target community	Positive media attention to bring in parents, staff, and funds
Our community has an appetite for funding this type of program		

phenomena that evidence shows are related to the larger, less easily measured phenomenon we are ultimately trying to measure.

Exhibit P, Programmatic Logic Model (below), offers a graphic illustration of such a model, using the child care example above. It is highly simplified, for our purposes, but you will get the idea. (Tool 24: Logic Model, on the CD, contains a blank worksheet.)

Programmatic Strategy in Action

In 2007 the Sierra Club decided that it needed to develop several new programmatic strategies to combat global climate change and contracted with La Piana Associates for help. Sierra Club leadership solicited ideas from its members and staff, asking for transformative ideas that build on the unique character of the Club, thus aiding its ongoing efforts at differentiation. The

Outputs	Short-term outcomes	Impact
6,000 days of service per year	80% of kids are reading-ready as they enter kindergarten 1 year after enrollment in our program	Kids succeed in school, beginning in kindergarten and carrying on throughout their elementary years, at higher rates than kids from families that did not receive a program such as ours
Develop a curriculum by the end of December		
400 hours of parent classes provided to a total of 20 families a year	90% of parents are reading to their kids nightly for 10 minutes after 1 year in our program	
The school will be full 85% of the days it operates		

Sierra Club convened a summit where a group of one hundred key leaders fleshed out and compared these and other ideas to one another. The leaders initially considered forty-four ideas for new programmatic strategies, but by the end of the summit, they had whittled them down to the eight ideas that the participants thought to be most promising. These ideas then underwent extensive testing from scientific, policy, fund development, and organizational feasibility perspectives. Essentially, the Club used a logic model approach to determine whether its top ideas would have their intended impact on global climate change; whether donors would support the ideas (these are big, aggressive, and therefore expensive ideas); and what organizational changes the Club would need to make to implement the ideas. The process need not be so formal as filling in a diagram; in this case the Club used a multiday gathering of leaders followed by intensive research by a staff and volunteer committee.

Throughout its fifty-year history, East Bay Agency for Children (EBAC) traditionally served school-age children who had mental health challenges. It then began a preschool program for four- and five-year-olds who had been abused, in an attempt to prevent the kinds of problems it was seeing in its six- to eight-year-old clients. Several years later EBAC determined that age four was still not optimal for early intervention. It then launched a parent-infant program as a bold attempt to help at-risk young mothers and their babies to get off on the right foot together. The new program's *assumption* was that in the early months after giving birth, a young mother is especially open to changing her life (for example, abandoning drugs, ending abusive relationships, and not perpetrating crime). They reasoned that providing a new mother with simple and compelling parent education and appropriate support in making changes would be the most effective interventions to produce a positive long-term impact.

The program's *activities* included home-based counseling and parent education for the mother, which led to a stronger parent-child bond (*short-term outcome*), and (it was hoped) eventually to breaking the cycle of abuse, poverty, and crime into which the mothers themselves typically had been born (*impact*).

Amnesty International USA was horrified by the idea of the United States deliberately sending prisoners to foreign jails in countries known for the practice of torture, and by the development of Guantanamo Bay as an extralegal prison from which there is no release and no access to the legal system.[33] It determined that the best way to combat these human rights abuses was to appeal to basic American decency and values. This *assumption* became the basis for Amnesty's "The America I Believe In" campaign. This campaign identifies abusive U.S. government practices as being outside of the traditional American value system. It employs a variety of media to convey the message (*activities*), hoping to build public opposition to these practices (*short-term outcomes*) leading eventually to their abolition (*impact*).

Programmatic Strategy Essentials

Using the programmatic logic model, you can address the essential elements of a successful programmatic strategy. These include the following questions.

1. **What programs should we offer?** What activities, and bundles of activities, are we uniquely qualified to deliver? The programs we offer must advance our mission, but they must also meet our own organizational needs for differentiation, strengthen our competitive advantage, and improve our ability to secure the resources necessary to deliver the programmatic activities in the first place. That is, *the programmatic choices you make in the middle of the Strategy Pyramid must support your organizational strategy choice made at the top.*

   To take an extreme example, a Humane Society opens a food pantry for humans (a worthy enough activity in itself). But this strategy does not play to the organization's strengths, nor use its accumulated expertise in animal care, nor strengthen the public's view of the Society as the best place for animal care. The new program also confuses the Society's core constituency of animal lovers and donors and distracts its board and management from their core mission. *Programmatic strategies must support organizational strategies.*

---

[33] Personal communication with client.

2. **Where should the programs be located?** The choice of location for delivery of a programmatic activity is intimately bound up with the activity itself. Is it critical for the activity to be within walking distance or near public transportation for its intended customers? Is there a special resource, such as the ocean, a historic building, or a performance venue that is essential to the activity? Should there be more than one location or a single fixed location augmented by "in the field" service delivery (e.g., in a needle exchange program)?

3. **Whom should the programs target?** In Chapter 4 we discussed target population, but within your organization you may have more specifically targeted subpopulations for different programs. For example, a community center may have one program targeting teens and another for seniors. It is critical to be clear about who the program is designed to engage and why. Advocacy organizations have perhaps the toughest time with this question. Amnesty International, for example, appeals to people who want to defend human rights at home and abroad, which may be the only thing its supporters have in common. The greater the diversity of your constituency, the harder you have to work to both understand their varying needs and provide them with a unified sense of belonging to or identifying with the organization.

4. **What approaches are most likely to succeed?** A wide range of options (in terms of your approach) can exist even within a fairly narrow scope of programmatic choices. If the organization's mission (the top of the Strategy Pyramid) is to promote the mental health of chronically homeless mentally ill adults, the organization still faces many programmatic strategy choices. Let's say it chooses to provide a drop-in treatment program (as opposed to a twenty-four-hour care program, an advocacy program, and so forth). The organization still must decide what kind of drop-in treatment it will provide. Will the program be run by consumers or professionally staffed? Will it emphasize the arts as a means of expression? This is a situation where reading the literature in a chosen field, visiting others who are doing similar work, and conferring with colleagues of all kinds are invaluable activities so that in the end you choose a programmatic model that both fits your organization and is strongly believed to work (will produce your desired outcomes).

5. **What are we mandated to do and what are we prohibited from doing?** While nonprofits enjoy a wide freedom within the scope of their tax exemption, there are limits. The broadest limits are legally imposed: the organization cannot go outside its exempt purpose (such as the Humane Society doing food pantry work). Practically speaking, the limits that concern you most are those provided by your bylaws and board, as well as those provided by any national federations or accreditation bodies you belong to. You must follow bylaws stating how you will operate: a local Girl Scouts Council must live by the rules provided by its charter from Girl Scouts USA. Those nonprofits that accept government funding agree to abide by a whole raft of additional rules ranging from how long to retain financial records to qualifications for board members to providing assurances not to help terrorists.

When to Form New Programmatic Strategies

As with organizational strategies, there is nothing magic about when to revisit your current programmatic strategy choices. Remember, however, that *programmatic choices,* when seen as strategies, are (to revive our earliest definition of strategy) an organized pattern of behavior toward an end. This means that if your programmatic choices (behavior) are no longer the optimal way of pursuing your mission (end), they should be changed. Sometimes new breakthroughs supersede programs, as in the example of drug therapy for depression mentioned earlier. Sometimes other organizations come into the market and do a better job of providing the activities you have long provided, taking your business away. Whatever the reason, changing programs is one of the toughest management challenges, since staff (and often volunteers and board members) are so closely identified with "the way things are done today."

Conclusion: **Programs As Strategic Choices**

The programmatic logic model is only a tool to be used in the service of finding an effective programmatic strategy. I like this particular tool, but there may be others you wish to employ for the same purpose. Remember, the logic model is not itself a substitute for a programmatic strategy. Remember, too, that programmatic strategy is in the middle of the Strategy Pyramid and must support the organizational strategy: your mission, business model, market awareness, and competitive advantage, as well as your branding and resource acquisition strategies.

Programmatic strategies pertain to how the organization carries out its mission. But, important as they are to an organization's success, they stand on the broad shoulders of operational strategies, which help an organization determine how best to manage a multitude of necessary tasks. This is the focus of our next chapter.

Chapter Eight:

Forming Operational Strategies

Excellence is doing ordinary things extraordinarily well.
— John W. Gardner[34]

IN THE STRATEGY PYRAMID, operational strategies form the broad base upon which rest the other forms of strategy. Operational strategies support organizational and programmatic strategies by providing a stable and well-functioning organizational foundation; they enable higher level strategies with minimal interference. The late John Gardner, one of the great leaders of our sector during the second half of the twentieth century, reminds us that so much of what we do in organizational life is "ordinary," but nonetheless essential. This chapter is about choosing the right ordinary things to do, and then doing them with excellence.

OPERATIONAL
Administer and oversee systems, policies, and personnel in areas such as finance, human resources, communications, and information technology

Operations occupy much of a nonprofit manager's time. A sound structure includes systems and processes for managing finances, raising money, recruiting and supervising paid and unpaid staff, developing the board, delivering programs, and communicating the organization's work. While many of the skills necessary to develop sound operational strategies are generic—for example, accounting skills or fundraising ability—it is a mistake to assume that any important operational system or policy can come directly from a cookie cutter.

---

[34] John W. Gardener as quoted at www.leader-values.com/Content/ detail.asp?ContentDetailID=228.

Remember that *strategy* is an organized pattern of behavior toward an end. In the realm of operational strategy, the behaviors—raising, managing, and spending money; recruiting, hiring, and training staff; or finding, developing, and managing facilities—must all pull toward a specific, not a generic, end: enhancing your organization's ability to advance its mission.

Think of the operational elements of your work as opportunities to form and reinforce your values as well as to perform necessary and routine functions. In fact, if not carefully tended, operations can oppose organizational values and thwart programmatic and organizational strategies. For example, some philanthropic foundations invest their funds in companies that thwart their philanthropic goals—such as funding antismoking programs while investing in Philip Morris, or funding gun control initiatives while owning stock in arms makers. There are an abundance of less dramatic opportunities to align your operational strategies with your programmatic strategies and even with your organizational strategies.

From Theory to Action:

Assessing Organizational Processes

A good place to start your consideration of operational strategy is by taking stock of your current processes. We have developed an array of tools for this purpose. One is aimed at mature organizations, another at start-up nonprofits, and still another is framed as a self-assessment process. These are all included on the CD.

▸ Tool 20: Mission Statement Refinement

▸ Tool 21: Organizational Self-Assessment and Discussion

▸ Tool 22: The Due Diligence Tool

▸ Tool 23: Opportunity Matrix

▸ Tool 24: Logic Model

▸ Tool 25: 90-Day Plan for Incremental Improvements

▸ Tool 26: Post-Action Debriefing

Real Life Operational Strategy

The Gates Foundation, criticized for investing in corporations whose products were in conflict with its work, responded by reviewing its investment policies.[35] It reaffirmed that the foundation, the largest private philanthropy in the world, would continue to avoid investments in tobacco companies, but beyond that prohibition it decided to let return on investment be its guide. This is a difficult decision because refusing to invest in certain companies can result in lower investment returns, hindering a foundation's ability to fund its programs. On the other hand, there is clearly some moral value—as Gates acknowledged with its no-tobacco policy—in refusing to invest in certain companies.

---

[35] Eisenberg, Pablo, "Gates: Role Model in Need of Remodeling," *Chronicle of Philanthropy* 19, no. 10 (March 8, 2007): pp. 39–41.

While such divestment is largely symbolic—even in the case of the enormous Gates Foundation—the choice of a financial strategy (an operational strategy) that supports rather than thwarts its mission (an organizational strategy) is valuable. If nothing else, the foundation now knows better why it will stick with this particular strategy: it has become more conscious of the reasoning behind its choice. Its financial (operational) strategy now aligns with its organizational strategy.

East Bay Agency for Children (EBAC) always invested in staff development. However, as its programs grew in number and complexity, individual professional development line items in each program budget were no longer the most efficient means of investing its limited resources devoted to this purpose. For example, a social worker from one program might attend a conference and, at best, report on what she learned to other staff in her own program. The rest of the organization learned nothing. EBAC decided to pool the professional development budgets from its ten programs into one larger line item. To manage this function it recruited a staff committee representing the programs. It was critical that the committee be small enough to function, while representing EBAC's different types of employees: social workers, psychologists, teachers, child care counselors, and others. The committee received complete authority over the professional development line item, and was told it could send individuals to conferences, bring in speakers, or organize in-house trainings as it felt best. Over the next few years, many unintended positive developments ensued from this new operational strategy. For example, in an effort to save money, the committee began a monthly series of Grand Rounds meetings where clinical staff from different departments presented cases. Similarly, when an outside trainer was hired, staff members from all programs were invited. Not only did this stretch EBAC's learning dollars across a wider array of staff members, but, by working and learning together, it increased communication among the ten program staffs. The committee, whose members changed each year, managed its budget diligently. In fact, this operational strategy actually saved the organization money while enhancing its learning.[36]

---

[36] Personal experience. I was EBAC's executive director when this occurred.

Operational Strategy Essentials

Here are some questions representing the typical concerns of operational strategy.

1. *What systems, policies, and processes do we need in order to be well-run and stable?*

   Even smaller nonprofits have multiple systems (accounting software, e-mail, a salary scale), policies (the mission statement, personnel policies, cash management policies), and processes (new client intake, staff performance reviews, creation of staff meeting agendas). The question is how to construct the best, most useful systems, policies, and processes—ones that staff will respect for their fairness and helpfulness, board members will find efficient and easily intelligible, and all stakeholders will feel enhance their experience of the organization. Poorly functioning systems can lead to bad data, leading in turn to a lack of information for management decision making, erroneous reports to funders, and other disasters. Poorly constructed—or absent—policies can lead to a range of bad outcomes, everything from a lack of clarity around expectations to lawsuits alleging negligence or capriciousness ("They had no personnel policy around performance, your honor; they just fired me for no reason!"). Poor processes lead to chaos and wasted effort as people need to reinvent the wheel each time they do what should be a routine task.

2. *What are our human, financial, and facilities resource requirements for the next year?*

   One very useful element of traditional strategic planning is the process of setting operational goals. The problem, as we have seen, is that these operational goals, which should be created to further your organizational strategies, can be mistaken for actual strategies. Each year your nonprofit must set a budget for the next twelve months, determine how many and what kind of staff it needs and can afford, and plan for facilities and other capital needs in the short and longer term. This essential budgeting and operational planning process should not be mistaken for the process of forming organizational strategies to address Big Questions. Rather, it should be undertaken with an understanding of those strategies and in support of them.

Many nonprofits create annual plans by simply rolling forward last year's budgets (for people, funds, and facilities), perhaps with a nod toward the ever-increasing cost of living. This process misses the very real need to connect planned activity levels to organizational strategies. For example, if you are faced with a new and serious competitive threat, it may be necessary to put more resources into marketing to maintain your position in customers' eyes. Simply rolling over last year's marketing budget may not be adequate. Trade-offs may be required to adequately fund marketing. These decisions will be easier for everyone to swallow if you have first worked out an organizational strategy that is widely accepted. Rather than a fight over the budget, everyone will then have better understanding of why difficult choices have to be made.

3. *What are our longer-term capital, staffing, and cash needs?*

Operational strategy is about more than the next year. Some longer-term operational needs can be reasonably anticipated and planned for. If you know you will need a new building for your growing programs within five years, you would be wise to begin planning for it now. Similarly, if predictable changes in your field mean that your staff will need extensive retraining to keep up with cutting-edge practice, you can begin planning now for an effort of several years' duration. If changes in your funding mix mean you will move over the next couple of years from a customer base that typically offers a thirty-day turnaround on payment of your invoices to a more complex one where payment, via intermediaries, is likely to take several months, you may decide to begin building your liquidity or establishing a line of credit now so that you will not face a cash crisis in two years. In each case, these longer-term needs can be addressed through operational strategies that get implemented year to year.

4. *What operational information do our leaders need to make good decisions?*

Ultimately, it is not good enough to have first-rate systems, policies, and processes if the information they produce is not available to decision makers in a timely way and in a useable form. Every nonprofit leader takes in information differently. Some want detailed financial information on their desk each week, and others prefer to let a finance specialist get into the details while they only monitor overall performance against budget. Some will write policy statements themselves, agonizing over every word of the employee manual, while others prefer to delegate this task and simply edit and approve someone else's work. Since your nonprofit is likely to have several people who need information produced from or about your operations (board members with varying degrees of financial sophistication, managers with different responsibilities, and funders with various reporting requirements), it is best to develop systems, policies, and processes with flexible reporting mechanisms and capabilities.

When to Form New Operational Strategies

As with organizational and programmatic strategies, so too with operational strategies: new strategies need to be created when the old ones no longer function optimally. For a smaller nonprofit, human resource functions are typically handled by the executive director, a bookkeeper, or even the receptionist, and financials may be created using Quicken. As the organization grows, these simple solutions give way to dedicated specialized staff and more powerful accounting software. Of course it is usually not wise to wait until a system, policy, or process is completely broken or outmoded before recognizing the need for an upgrade in functioning, so some degree of anticipation and planning is best.

Usually operational strategies decline in usefulness gradually. On the organizational strategy level you may wake up one day to find that a new competitor is stealing your thunder; on the programmatic strategy level you may read something in a professional journal that is going to completely change your approach to your mission; but you are likely to have plenty of notice when an operational strategy is beginning to fail. For example,

- Funders begin asking for more detail in your financial reports than your current system can provide, leading to a time-consuming process of creating the desired reports manually.

- Your tried-and-true monthly in-service training session for staff is attended by fewer and fewer of the people whom you think could most benefit from developing some new skills.

- Your board is asking for a monthly report on services provided that requires each program to submit data to a central point where someone else turns it into the report format the board wants.

- Your staff are unhappy, morale is low, and you believe your middle-management program leaders are not prepared to provide adequate supervision and support to the front line.

None of these situations is likely to spring fully formed onto the scene all at once; they develop slowly, but inexorably. Most need not be fixed immediately. You are probably aware right now of various systems, policies, and processes that are gradually becoming less useful to your organization. However, due to limited time and funds, you may reasonably choose to ignore these issues for the time being, or work on only one area at a time while anxiously monitoring the decline of the temporarily neglected others. This gradual approach to upgrades and replacements is both natural and necessary as you try to wring the last ounce of utility out of a previous investment before needing to make a new one.

Conclusion: **Operations Are the Broad Shoulders of Strategy**

Thinking of operational decisions as contributing to operational strategies helps us to see both their relationship with one another and their essential role in the service of programmatic and organizational strategies. Operational strategies are the systems, policies, and processes you use to manage the day-to-day functions of your organization in support of programmatic and organizational strategies. As noted earlier, operational strategies are the broad shoulders upon which rest programmatic strategies, and eventually, organizational strategies. They are also the tools you use to plan for the next year's deployment of resources and to anticipate and plan for longer-term resource needs.

Chapter Nine:
Putting It All Together

> Leaders don't create followers, they create more leaders.
>
> —Tom Peters[37]

Using Real-Time Strategic Planning to Advance Your Mission and Vision

Leadership is all about strategy, and strategy is all about leadership. Leaders sometimes inspire, push, or cajole their organizations toward new strategies, while at other times they skip all of that and just announce the new strategy as a *fait accompli*. But strategies can only succeed if there is sufficient will and skill—at the leadership level and throughout the organization—to implement them successfully. Real-Time Strategic Planning is a great tool both for education and persuasion on the one hand, and for moving implementation forward on the other.

The essential task of leadership, as Tom Peters reminds us, is not to turn people into followers, but to help them to become leaders in their own right. At the heart of that process is education. People need information, and the tools to make sense of it, to become good leaders. This task is also aided by helping them to understand and use the processes described in Real-Time Strategic Planning and all that they entail. A constant theme in this book has been the need to engage a wide variety of organizational stakeholders in your deliberative processes: to ask their opinions, engage

---

[37] Tom Peters, as quoted at www.thepracticeofleadership.net/2007/08/19/tom-peters-on-leadership.

them in debates, or assign them market research tasks. Along the way, they will come to form their own opinions about where the organization should go, based on experience and facts, not preformed ideas. When this happens you will have many lively debates, but you will also have a healthier organization that is more keenly focused on pursuit of its mission in the most effective manner you can collectively determine.

Strategy Formation As a Continuous Cycle

We first learned about the notion of strategy formation as a cycle in the opening of Chapter 4, and subsequently we explored each step on the Real-Time Strategic Planning Cycle. Strategy formation is best thought of as a continuous cycle that contrasts with the episodic three-year cycle used in traditional planning. The nature and timing of your efforts will be unique to your organization and its situation. But the process steps in the ongoing cycle are fairly predictable, and they tie organizational, programmatic, and operational strategies into a neat bundle. Let's take one final look at the Real-Time Strategic Planning Cycle (Exhibit Q), to revisit how these processes tie together.

Study the Real-Time Strategic Planning Cycle. Starting with the outer ring of arrows, you will occasionally ask the "Who are we?" questions. These include a review of your mission, if necessary, followed by a review of your business model, which often involves articulating it for the first time. Next comes an in-depth consideration of your market, described in Chapter 4. Pay special attention to your competitive situation in the market. As you move through these considerations, you also move from "Who are we?" to "Where are we and how did we get here?"—from knowing who you are to understanding your position in the world. This process flows naturally and is needed periodically, when any part of your current understanding is becoming dated or you think it may be wrong for your current or anticipated future situation. The Real-Time Strategic Planning process described in Chapters 4 and 5 quickly takes you through the entire process and rolls up your learning about yourself and your market into an *identity statement,* a description of all the things that shape your organization in the environment. Its value lies in the conscious work done to research or surface the organization's identity so that when the organization is presented with an opportunity or threat, it can act with self-knowledge.

EXHIBIT Q Real-Time Strategic Planning Cycle

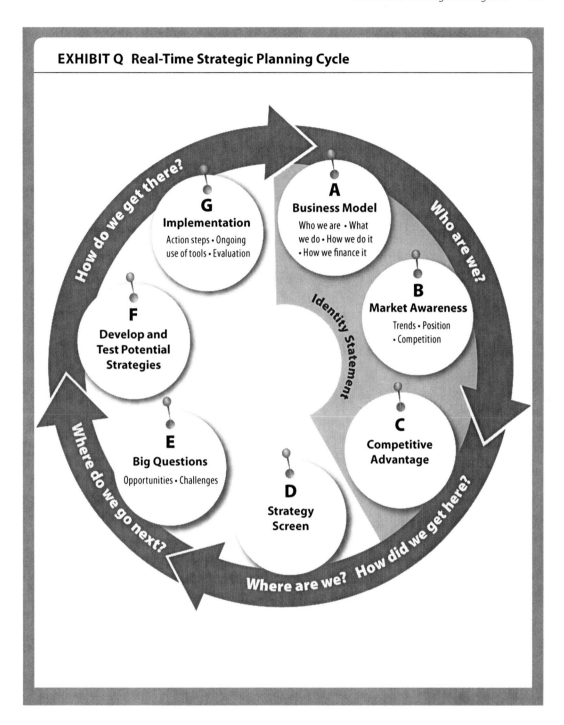

This statement is summed up, in part, by the criteria expressed in the Strategy Screen, which you developed in Chapter 5. It has prepared your organization to tackle the next set of challenges: "Where do we go next, and how do we get there?" Use these processes to respond to Big Questions, which are either opportunities or challenges facing your organization (described in Chapter 6). This is really the heart of Real-Time Strategic Planning, and includes testing out different potential strategies, choosing one, and then implementing it.

The entire Real-Time Strategic Planning Cycle need not be followed in any particular time frame. However, it usually flows more or less in the direction and fashion outlined here. Your organization will follow its own course, and at times will vary from the cycle shown. The programmatic and operational strategies you choose will be most effective if they are consciously constructed to advance and reinforce your programmatic strategies.

Crafting a "Traditional" Strategic Plan

It is preferable to continuously monitor the organization's environment and respond immediately to new Big Questions with appropriate strategies. The nonprofit strategy revolution is all about quickly converting thought to action in real time in order to address opportunities and challenges in a rapid-response world. But what if your funders or board are still asking "Where is the strategic plan?" Here's a story that will go a long way toward answering this question.

> A few years ago I undertook an unusual engagement. A major foundation asked a well-known nonprofit to consider taking on an important piece of work that was, strictly speaking, not within its normal scope. Still, there were good reasons for this funder's request, and for the nonprofit to accept the offer. My consulting team had ten weeks to work with the nonprofit to develop a new strategy and then to determine whether this new strategy made sense. We deeply engaged the board and staff; interviewed lots of stakeholders, competitors, and other funders; and took the organization through several of the processes described in this book.
>
> In the end, the organization decided to accept the funder's offer. The organization prepared a grant proposal describing the processes we went through, the program the organization proposed to carry out with the funds, and the deliverables. It was a good solid piece of work put together by the organization's executive

director, with information provided in part by our consulting team. However, soon after submitting the proposal the executive director received a call from a program officer at the foundation. The proposal looked good; it was just what the funder had hoped for. There was just one catch: the funder required all grant proposals of this size to be accompanied by a strategic plan. Where was the strategic plan?

The executive director correctly explained to the program officer that the entire proposal was the result of an intense strategy consideration and that, in fact, the whole new thrust of the organization was the result of this process. The program officer's response: "Yes, but where is the strategic plan? I have the proposal, but I need to have on file your strategic plan."

The executive director called me, a bit frantic. The completed proposal package was due by 5 PM and would not be able to go on the funder's next docket unless it was considered complete by day's end. I looked at my watch—it was 10 AM. "No problem," I said. We pulled out a traditional strategic plan template like the one contained in Step 4 of Exhibit A (page 9), and over the phone we talked our way through it. The executive director then got off the phone, wrote the "strategic plan" in about three hours, and submitted it on time. The grant was approved.

The point of this anecdote is that first and foremost you need to use the processes that work for you when faced with Big Questions, but that you can pretty easily translate those processes and decisions into a traditional strategic plan *document* if necessary. Knowing where you are going and why is essential; the *way* it gets portrayed and written up is optional.

From Theory to Action:

Writing a Strategic Plan

Funders, boards, and others are not going to quit demanding to see your traditional strategic plan simply because we've declared a revolution. Tool 10: Strategy Road Map, in Part 2, ties all the pieces of the process you went through into a document that may (and we hope with time increasingly will) satisfy funders requiring such a plan. If you are concerned that the road map will not meet the demands of those counter-revolutionaries (who often, after all, influence a significant portion of your budget), we suggest using the strategic plan template from Bryan Barry's classic *Strategic Planning Workbook for Nonprofit Organizations.** This template has been adapted and included on the CD.

▸ Tool 10: Strategy Road Map (page 159)

▸ Tool 27: Traditional Strategic Plan Template (on CD)

---

* Bryan W. Barry, *Strategic Planning Workbook for Nonprofit Organizations, Revised and Updated* (Saint Paul, MN: Fieldstone Alliance, 1997).

Traditional strategic planning is not a useless activity in itself. It has simply been made to perform too many functions, many of which it is ill-suited to accomplish. Organizations that use Real-Time Strategic Planning may then go on to use aspects of traditional strategic planning—in a truncated and more effective way—to turn their strategies into goals. This is fine. What's important is to find strategies that advance your mission, and then ensure that you get there. That in itself is revolutionary.

And speaking of revolutionaries, as promised at the outset, now that you have completed this workbook, you have earned a Nonprofit Strategy Revolutionary Certificate. You can download it from the CD accompanying this book.

Conclusion: **Real-Time Strategy in a Rapid-Response World**

The future is famously unpredictable, except for death and taxes. To that pair of givens I would add a third: change. Constant change is the primary driver of the nonprofit strategy revolution. We do not have the luxury of expensive year-long strategic planning exercises, especially when their impact on the organization's direction is usually so slight. Try out the tools and thought processes contained in this book. Our clients have, and they report that these ways of thinking about strategy are valuable—at least by the measure that they keep hiring us to do more of it! The following quote from a report by our outside evaluator, Jim Thomas, illustrates one type of benefit organizations have gained by using the approach I have recommended:

> In a number of the pilot cases, the participants came to an important new view of the identity of the organization. Frequently, this happened during the strategy formation session,[38] but in some cases it continued to develop over a period of months, even without consultant contact. Participants say that they came to see "who" they are as an organization in a new and meaningful way. Participants with different roles in the organization and with different levels of experience and knowledge about the organization, through the

---

[38] During our research, we used the phrase "strategy formation" to describe the process. As we formalized our research into this book, we developed the term Real-Time Strategic Planning to convey that the process was a form of planning, but that unlike traditional planning, it occurred quickly and as needed.

strategy formation process, begin to have a more unified and strategic vision of the organization. The executive director of a relatively young organization put it this way:

"First, [strategy formation] brought our board into a lot more focus about the organization so that it did not all have to come from me. At the time of the session we had people who had previously been on an advisory board and we had brand new board members. So it was a mix of people at different stages with the organization, and there had never been an opportunity for all of us to come together about our understanding of the organization and our vision for it. The session brought us, board and staff, to look at all of that.

"The second thing [strategy formation] did was that it opened up new and different opportunities for us in terms of funding. As we started talking together about who we are—doing our identity statement—we started having different ideas about what we could do. It was like we got a clearer view of what to look for. Then, while we still had our heads together, we thought of new sources for funding for these ideas. It has turned out well."

Sound strategic thinking can breathe new life into a stumbling nonprofit organization; it can help a successful one avoid unseen pitfalls and move toward even greater ability to serve its mission; and it can show a nonprofit at a crossroads in its development where the best path ahead lies. We have seen these outcomes with our clients and with some of the pilots in our research effort. We have also seen them in more traditional strategy engagements over the years. So why prescribe the processes we have just described? In one sense, the value in Real-Time Strategic Planning, the approach recommended by the nonprofit strategy revolution, is that it makes sense—it works with the way successful nonprofit leaders think and with their preference for thoughtful action over long, deliberative processes. It does not require an exceptionally talented consultant or a series of customized shortcuts to the traditional strategic planning approach. It is intuitive, and therefore accessible to every nonprofit leader.

Strategy is a habit of mind. I have described new habits of thinking about strategy in a nonprofit and offered a detailed process for forming both a clearer sense of your organization's identity (the identity statement), and for creating responses to Big Questions. Part 2 of this book offers a step-by-step practical guide to working with the Real-Time Strategic Planning process.

In the course of our research we have also adapted (and in some cases invented) a multitude of tools and processes that you can use to advance and enhance your organization's strategic thinking capability, often on an ongoing basis, as well as to deal with a particular question. These tools are included on the CD accompanying this book.

PART **TWO**

Essential Tools for Forming Strategy

Essential Tools for Forming Strategy

The tools contained in this section are useful in helping a nonprofit to identify and address the critical strategic issues it faces. Used together, they are the backbone of our one-day strategy formation process, which usually kicks off a Real-Time Strategic Planning process. To organize and conduct such a session, see the Facilitator's Guide to Real-Time Strategic Planning on the CD accompanying this book. Each of the ten tools provided here in Part 2 may be of use to you independently as well.

Blank versions of these tools, suitable for printing or filling in electronically, are provided on the CD accompanying this book.

CURRENT BUSINESS MODEL

This tool helps an organization to define its business model. It answers these questions:

1. Where (in what geographic area) do we provide our services?

2. Who do we serve? (Who are our primary stakeholders, i.e., our customers?)

3. How do we serve them? (What programs/services do we offer?)

4. What sources of funding do we rely on to fund our work?

It also helps the group to make explicit what its business model does not include: what geographic areas it does not serve, what customers it does not target, what services it does not provide, and what sources of funding it does not have or does not seek.

Use, outcomes, and measures

SITUATION: When is this tool useful?	OUTCOMES: How will you know you've achieved your goals?
Defining your business model is useful when your nonprofit . . . • Is considering a new program or new direction, or perceives a competitive threat to its current business • Is considering a merger or other partnership and needs to clarify areas of overlap with its potential partner(s) • Has new board members and/or staff • Uses it as an orientation tool • Operates in silos (people do not work or communicate across organizational boundaries)	Indicators and measures of outcomes: • A strong sense of the organization's current position in the marketplace • A clear idea of how the partnership may impact your current business model, and hence your mission • A better understanding of the nonprofit's business model • The answers to the "where," "who," "how," and "what" questions (above) and also the choices that have been made about what the organization does not do • Everyone is on the same page in their understanding; each person has an increased sense of being part of the whole organization

How should you use it?

This tool is an integral component of the Real-Time Strategic Planning kick-off session as described in the Facilitator's Guide (on the accompanying CD). It can also be used by itself outside of the Real-Time Strategic Planning process. Either way, it is best completed by a group of board and staff who participate in answering each of the questions. This helps bring out decisions that may not be obvious. It may also reveal decisions that are no longer valid due to changes in the external environment and so need to be reconsidered. If the organization has many different services targeting many different customers, the "current scope" may need to be defined service-by-service. This process can reveal whether there is dissonance in the organization's scope, such as a program that does not really serve the mission, but reflects "scope creep" (sometimes a result of chasing funds).

WORKSHEET 1.1 **Current Business Model** (Sample)

Scope	Includes	Does <u>not</u> include
Geographic service area	All four counties in our region	Any areas outside of our region
Customers served	+ Adults ages 18–64 + Both men and women + Families of clients (where appropriate) + With selected disorders: • Schizophrenia • Major depression • Forensic • Mental health and substance abuse	- Anyone under age 18 or age 65+ - Diagnosis of substance abuse only - Developmentally disabled (DD) - Mental health and DD - With private insurance
Programs / Services offered	+ Case management + Short- and long-term housing + Outreach to homeless + Day treatment + Respite care	- Crisis intervention - Outpatient services - Adolescent services - Services for aging - Acute inpatient facility
Funding sources	Current sources of funding and why we pursue these sources: + Our primary source of funding is government sources; we serve public-pay clients (See also financial worksheets)	Funding sources we do not have or seek: - Corporations

FINANCIAL ANALYSIS

The Financial Analysis Tool consists of two one-page worksheets that together provide a snapshot of a nonprofit's financial situation. The first, Worksheet 2.1: Funding Sources, helps answer these questions:

1. What is our overall budget?

2. How diverse is our funding?

3. How much do we rely on particular sources of funding?

4. How has our funding changed (current compared to prior fiscal year)?

5. What changes do we expect in the coming fiscal year?

6. How stable are we? (Are we operating at a surplus or deficit, and if so, how large is it?)

The Program Income and Expenses Worksheet provides a picture of how revenue is allocated by program and by source (such as foundation grants, government funding, earned income, and so on). It helps answer these questions:

1. How is our income distributed across our programs?

2. Are any programs overly dependent on one source of income?

3. Are any sources of income at risk, thereby putting any programs at risk?

4. Are any programs running at a deficit?

This tool makes the nonprofit's financial situation very easy to grasp by board members.

Use, outcomes, and measures

SITUATION: When is this tool useful?	OUTCOMES: How will you know you've achieved your goals?
Financial analysis is useful when your nonprofit . . . • Wants to ensure that board members understand its financial situation • Needs to quickly convey key financial information (e.g., to new board members) • Wants a framework for examining trends in funding and considering their future impact • Needs to identify programs at risk and those with potential for growth	Indicators and measures of outcomes: • Knowledge of the nonprofit's financial situation and ability to engage in discussion about it; awareness of trends and needed actions • Increased awareness of organization's financial situation; ability to make informed decisions • Identification of current trends; analysis of future trends • Input into forming strategies for fund development

How should you use it?

This tool is a core component of the Real-Time Strategic Planning kick-off session, but it can also be used as a stand-alone tool. The worksheets, which are self-explanatory, should be completed by your organization's financial person or executive director. The first two columns of the Funding Sources Worksheet ask for the total revenue for the prior and current fiscal years. This total is then broken down into the sources (or types) of funding, shown as percentages to easily identify the contributions from each source, the diversity of funding sources, and changes from the prior to the current year. The worksheet also asks you to explain changes in levels and sources of funding and to indicate whether it is breaking even. You are also asked to identify any expected changes in funding sources and levels for the coming year. Regardless of your situation, this tool helps you to identify challenges or opportunities related to your financial status and to use this information in shaping action.

WORKSHEET 2.1 Funding Sources (Sample)

This worksheet displays your nonprofit's sources of revenue. This will help you review recent trends in funding (past and current fiscal years) and consider whether your nonprofit has sufficient diversity of funding. Additionally, by identifying which sources of funding are stable and what new sources of funding you might attract in the coming fiscal year(s), you will get a sense of your nonprofit's overall financial stability. The worksheet also asks you to enter your nonprofit's total revenue and expenses for each fiscal year, and to indicate whether you had a surplus, deficit, or neither.

Source of Revenue (income)	Percent of total budget last fiscal year	Percent of total budget current fiscal year	Comments (such as regarding changes in funding from prior to current year)	Comments regarding next fiscal year (such as changes in current funding sources in next fiscal year, new funding anticipated, funding at risk)
Foundation grants	5%	3%	Expect to increase this fiscal year	We will put more emphasis here; will hire a fund development expert
Corporate grants	0%	0%	No change	We don't want to spread ourselves too thin; this is not a likely source for us so we won't pursue it now
Government funding	85%	87%	No significant change	No significant change
Unrestricted funding (such as endowment, donors, memberships)	0%	0%	No change	No change
Earned income (including program fees)	10%	10%	No change	Would like to increase funding from this source
Total revenue	$5 million	$5.5 million		Similar to current year
Total expenses	$4.8 million	$5 million		Similar to current year
Surplus/(Deficit)	$200,000	$500,000		

1 2 3 4 5 6 7 8 9 10

WORKSHEET 2.2 Program Income and Expenses (Sample)

This worksheet asks you to examine how your nonprofit's revenue (income) is allocated and used by each main program area.

If your nonprofit has more than one main program area, please complete this worksheet (copy it if you have more than three main program areas). If you have only one program, skip this worksheet. It is intended to help you learn whether one or more of your programs are dependent on certain types of funding. If so, and if that type of funding is increasing, this will be positive for the program. If that type of funding is decreasing, this could pose risk for the program's future.

Source of Revenue (income)	Program = Housing (all residential combined)		Program = Case Management		Program = Psychosocial Rehabilitation	
	Income for program from each funding source ($)	% of total income from this source of funding allocated to this program	Income for program from each funding source ($)	% of total income from this source of funding allocated to this program	Income for program from each funding source ($)	% of total income from this source of funding allocated to this program
Foundation grants					$165,000	3%
Corporate grants						
Government funding	$4,000,000	73%	$750,000	13%	$35,000	1%
Unrestricted funding (such as endowment, donors, memberships)						
Earned income (including program fees)			$250,000	5%	$300,000	5%

(continued on next page)

Other

Source of Revenue (income)	Program = Housing (all residential combined)		Program = Case Management		Program = Psychosocial Rehabilitation	
	Income for program from each funding source ($)	% of total income from this source of funding allocated to this program	Income for program from each funding source ($)	% of total income from this source of funding allocated to this program	Income for program from each funding source ($)	% of total income from this source of funding allocated to this program
Total program income	$4 million	73%	$1 million	18%	$500,000	9%
Total program expenses (including admin. surplus/deficit)	$3 million		$1,250,000		$750,000	
Comments: Is the program too dependent on any source(s) of funding? Is funding at risk? Growing?	Yes—100% government funding No—in-demand service No—stable		Yes—insufficient reimbursement No—in-demand service Perhaps—with increased demand		Yes—insufficient reimbursement Services have decreased in demand in 3 of our counties, but increased in the largest county in our service area	

COMPETITOR ANALYSIS

The Competitor Analysis Tool compares your nonprofit to other organizations in your market competing for the same resources. The comparison focuses on key areas important to market success, and helps you identify your nonprofit's strengths and those of competitors. It also reveals areas where your nonprofit may want or need to strengthen its organizational capacity. This comparison helps clarify your nonprofit's competitive advantage, which is at the core of its identity.

Use, outcomes, and measures

A nonprofit should always be aware of other organizations in its market and know how it compares to them. The completed Competitor Analysis Worksheet should be reviewed and updated periodically, such as quarterly, or as competitors enter and exit the market or change their strategies. Specific situations where this tool is useful are listed below.

SITUATION: When is this tool useful?	OUTCOMES: How will you know you've achieved your goals?
Competitor analysis is useful when your nonprofit . . .	Indicators and measures of outcomes:
• Needs to develop an understanding of the external environment and its "market position"	• Better understanding of where the organization is positioned and a stronger foundation for development of strategy
• Wants to determine whether to expand to new markets (geographic, programmatic, and/or customers)	• Improved decision making
• Is considering partnering with another organization	• Greater awareness of the market; more proactive decision making
• Is in a very competitive and rapidly changing environment	

How should you use it?

The Competitor Analysis Tool focuses on the nonprofit's strongest direct and substitutable competitors, and consists of two main components: research and discussion or analysis. The research phase includes completing the Competitor Analysis Worksheet for your own nonprofit and its top three competitors prior to the session.* This phase may be as simple as asking staff and board members to share any knowledge they have of the competition. Or it may be more involved, encompassing online research (review of web sites) or primary research (surveys, interviews, or focus groups). A good first step is to ask board and staff members to complete the tool separately, drawing on their own knowledge, and then have them meet to discuss their findings.

The tool is designed to help nonprofits consider their competition from the standpoint of the resources they compete for: customers, media publicity, human resources, and funding. It encourages organizations to consider their competitors' strengths, and thus helps avoid the natural tendency to dismiss competitors by focusing on their weaknesses.

When we lead this discussion in our Real-Time Strategic Planning sessions, we often ask participants, "What do you admire about each competitor?" The far-right column of the worksheet is used to summarize the comparison, highlighting your nonprofit's strengths and areas needing improvement.

Once the Competitor Analysis Worksheet has been completed, the Competitive Advantage Handout (pages 136–137) can be used to help board and staff members clarify how the organization distinguishes itself from others.

* If your nonprofit has many competitors, you may decide to profile more than three competitors and to rank them in order of competitive position. If your nonprofit has few direct competitors, you should consider substitutable competitors such as those with services that are not directly comparable to yours but meet the same needs. For example, if your nonprofit produces live theater you may compete with movie theaters, rental DVDs, TV, and so forth for customers.

WORKSHEET 3.1 Competitor Analysis (Sample)

Complete this worksheet for your top three competitors and also for your nonprofit. Think about the competitor's strengths and weaknesses in each category. How strong a competitor is this? How does your nonprofit compare with each competitor in each area? Is it stronger than others, or not as strong?

Resource	What makes your nonprofit strong in this area? Our Nonprofit	What makes these competitors strong in this area? Competitor A	Competitor B	Competitor C	How does your nonprofit compare?
Organizations:					
Customers (such as number of customers, customer satisfaction, customer retention)	1,500 Satisfaction = 90% (based on customer surveys)	2,000 Satisfaction: Not sure, but we have heard generally good things about them; good quality, but high prices	1,200 Satisfaction: Due to customer complaints about quality, they have gotten negative press in local papers	800 Satisfaction: Our staff who have friends who work at "C" tell us they hear good things about the facility and the care	Good
Media attention or publicity	Better than most; positive	Good	Not good; negative (see above)	Average	Better than others

(continued on next page)

Worksheet 3.1 Competitor Analysis (Sample–continued)

Resource / Organizations:	What makes your nonprofit strong in this area? Our Nonprofit	What makes these competitor strong in this area? Competitor A	Competitor B	Competitor C	How does your nonprofit compare?
Human resources					
Staff	Committed/invested	Motivated by money, but good clinically	No so good clinically	Experienced; loyal	Good-fair
Board	Committed/invested	N/A	Weak; not providing good oversight	High-profile CEO	Excellent
Volunteers	Very few	N/A	Info not available	A lot	This area needs to be addressed
Funding					
Diversity of funding	Includes federal, state, and county money, United Way, trusts, foundations	Has more government sources (including Medicaid funding) than we do; has private pay	Has other funding not related to mental health	Government funding	Similar to others
Availability/ amount/types of funding	We are very reliant on government funding		Similar to our operating budget	Funding is secure	

(continued on next page)

Worksheet 3.1 Competitor Analysis (Sample–continued)

Resource	What makes your nonprofit strong in this area?	What makes these competitors strong in this area?			How does your nonprofit compare?
Organizations:	**Our Nonprofit**	**Competitor A**	**Competitor B**	**Competitor C**	
Programs or services (type, quality, number of services provided)	Residential focus, homeless expertise, good case management services	Clinical expertise, data system/IT expertise	Nonresidential Quality issues (see above)	Focus on residential; good clinical quality	We need more diversity; increased clinical
Mission-related impact	Very good	Not clear since it is a for-profit	Not clear; variable services and quality issues	On target	Very good
Comments	Long history, good reputation, collaborative approach	Not collaborative, reputation is that they are driven by profit	Lost credibility due to quality issues; still trying to regain prior reputation	Residential is its strong point	Good—strong; solid agency, well-established, deep local ties

(continued on next page)

Your nonprofit's competitive advantage is one of the most important—if not the most important—components of its strategy.

Definition

Competitive advantage is the ability to produce social value (have an impact, make a difference) by

- Using a unique asset (such as a strength that no other similar organization in your geographic area has), and/or

- Having outstanding execution (such as being faster or less expensive, or having better service, than other similar organizations in your geographic area)

  (See the next page for more information on these two types of competitive advantage.)

However, having a competitive advantage is not enough to be successful; an organization must understand and use its competitive advantage.

Discussion

Competitive advantage is determined, in part, through comparison of your nonprofit with its competitors. It is something that customers and funders value.

Your nonprofit's competitive advantage distinguishes it from others, thus allowing it to compete effectively for resources and customers.

If your nonprofit's mission reflects its social value, then its competitive advantage includes things that allow it to have a greater impact and a more positive outcome from its efforts.

Your nonprofit will only be successful in contributing true social value if it identifies and applies its competitive advantage.

Note: A nonprofit may have more than one competitive advantage; these may be specific to the situation for which it is forming a strategy. For example, suppose your nonprofit is a primary health care clinic serving low-income families. If immigrants to your service area are increasingly monolingual in Spanish, the fact that your organization has bicultural and bilingual staff (and your competitors do not) is a competitive advantage in serving this population. Also, if you are located on a main bus line and your competitors are not within easy reach of public transportation, your clinic is thus more accessible to the entire population and can draw clients from a broad geographic area.

Types of competitive advantage

Asset advantages

- Better program design leading to better outcomes
- Unique attributes of programs or services such as linguistic or cultural capacity
- An accessible location or network of locations
- An attractive or specialized building or property that enhances program delivery
- A robust, diversified funding base that provides flexibility and stability
- Great name recognition and reputation among funders and constituents
- Powerful partnerships
- A well-connected board of directors

Execution advantages

- Lower costs to funders or customers
- Greater efficiency in delivering programs or services per dollar spent
- Faster delivery of programs or services (e.g., no waiting for service)
- Sound marketing and communications that raise visibility and awareness
- Better accountability and public reporting

TREND ANALYSIS

Trend analysis involves examining external trends that impact your non-profit and, specifically, the resources that it depends on to be successful and sustainable. Trends primarily fall into two categories: those that impact your current and future customers (e.g., changing demographics and needs) and those that impact your current and future funding (e.g., changes in the economy and funders' priorities). This tool helps you to identify and analyze these trends, and determine their impact on your nonprofit. Trend analysis is important to organizational strategy.

Use, outcomes, and measures

Our world demands rapid responses. So, an organization that thinks and acts strategically is proactive and nimble. This requires the organization to be aware of trends in its market and their impact. Review and update the completed Trend Analysis Worksheet periodically as changes occur in the environment.

SITUATION: When is this tool useful?	OUTCOMES: How will you know you've achieved your goals?
A trend analysis is useful when your nonprofit . . . • Is in a market characterized by change in demographics, socioeconomic factors, needs of customers, priorities of funders, technology, policies, programmatic approaches, and levels of market competition • Has experienced an unanticipated change in its resources (such as a decline in customers or decreased funding) • Is aware of trends that will impact its market position and has identified one or more Big Question(s) that it must address	Indicators and measures of outcomes: • Better knowledge of the external environment and greater understanding of its potential impact on the organization • Greater sense of control over the situation • Identification of trends before they are "old news" • Improved decision-making capacity • Better understanding of the reasons for the changes • Better ability to forecast the impact of the changes • Identification of actions to reduce negative and increase positive impact • Improved decision making and formation of effective strategies to address Big Questions • Reduction of projected negative impact

How should you use it?

Similar to Tool 3: Competitor Analysis, a trend analysis consists of two main components: research and discussion or analysis. The research phase focuses on completing the Trend Analysis Worksheet by identifying the key current and future trends that may impact your nonprofit and, specifically, its ability to secure the resources it needs. This research can be as simple as asking staff and board members, based on their own knowledge, to identify key market trends using the Trend Analysis Worksheet as a framework.

Or it may be more involved. For example, you may extend your research to a review of trusted web sites (such as the Foundation Center's Philanthropy News Digest),* key nonprofit sector publications (such as the *Chronicle of Philanthropy* and the *Nonprofit Quarterly*), publications focused on your particular subsector, and your local newspapers. Several of the tools presented in this workbook can help you to proactively identify and analyze trends, including Tool 14: Strategic Thinkers Group; Tool 15: Expert Interviews, and Tool 17: Brainstorming Process. Tool 3: Competitor Analysis, conducted over time, is also helpful in identifying market trends.

We suggest you ask staff and board members complete the Trend Analysis Worksheet on their own prior to the Real-Time Strategic Planning kick-off session and then come together to discuss their thoughts. This variety of perspectives, experiences, and backgrounds provides the foundation for a rich discussion. The analysis of the trends helps identify any Big Questions facing the nonprofit and provides guidance in forming strategies to address them.

On an ongoing basis, the nonprofit should keep its eyes and ears open to trends in the environment, using research tools such as those mentioned above. This does not require a lot of time; most important is being on the lookout for information as you go about your normal routine: read your local papers, talk with community leaders, attend conferences, and chat with your colleagues. Set aside time at staff and board meetings to share your findings and discuss their implications.

* Philanthropy News Digest, http://foundationcenter.org/pnd.

WORKSHEET 4.1 **Trend Analysis** (Sample)

Complete the worksheet below. If you know your market well, through discussion you and your colleagues should be able to do it off the top of your heads. For each trend, identify the direction of the trend as it applies to your nonprofit's environment. Is it increasing, decreasing, staying about the same? In the comments column include the sources you used, if any, to identify and analyze this trend. How reliable are these sources? To prepare for the trend analysis discussion, consider: How important is this trend to your nonprofit? What do you think your nonprofit needs to do to address this trend?

Type of trends	Direction of trend	Comments
Social needs or demands for your programs or services	Needs or demands are ☑ Increasing ☐ Decreasing ☐ Staying about the same	Residential and case management services will be high priority for government funding. The influencing factors are federal compliance and the growing concern over homelessness.
Available funding for your programs or services	Funding is ☐ Increasing ☐ Decreasing ☑ Staying about the same	
Other trends impacting your organization	The lack of young people entering the sector and the exodus of seasoned leaders is causing a growing leadership deficit.	Our well-respected and excellent founder is retiring in 2 years. It may be difficult to replace her.

FUTURE BUSINESS MODEL

The Future Business Model Tool is the companion tool to Tool 1: Current Business Model. The difference is that it asks your group to look forward into the future to determine where you want to go based on the needs of your customers and other market conditions.

After the group has defined its current scope and business model, prioritized its key competitors, identified its competitive advantages (if any), and analyzed current and future trends and their impact, it is ready to consider its future scope and business model. For example, competitive pressures, demographic shifts, or funding changes may cause the organization to rethink its current business model to react to expected trends. Using this tool, the group answers these questions:

1. In what geographic area might we provide our services? Where might we expand?

2. Who might we serve? What customers might we expand to serve?

3. How might we serve them? What additional services might we offer?

4. What sources of funding will we rely on? What sources will we seek?

5. Equally important, this tool helps the group to identify and make explicit what its future business model will not include.

Use, outcomes, and measures

SITUATION: When is this tool useful?	OUTCOMES: How will you know you've achieved your goals?
Defining your future business model is useful when your nonprofit . . . • Is faced with trends that may impact its customer base, funding sources, or types of services offered • Is considering a new strategy and needs to know how this will impact its current business model and its identity • Needs to clarify what areas its business model will exclude in the future to avoid confusion	Indicators and measures of outcomes: • Consensus on what actions the nonprofit will take to address these trends and clarity on what needs to be explored further to make these changes • Clarity about the impact on future business model and identity • Explicit definition of a business model; shared understanding of decisions

TOOL ① ② ③ ④ ⑤ ⑥ ⑦ ⑧ ⑨ ⑩

How should you use it?

An integral part of the Real-Time Strategic Planning kick-off session, this tool can also be used outside of that process—alone or as part of another strategy formation process. It should be used following Tool 1: Current Business Model. The process is the same as for the latter: completed by a group of board and staff where all participate in answering each of the questions and followed by an open, facilitated discussion with reflection on the implications of any deviations from the current business model. Those changes that are not certain should be included in Tool 9: Next Steps Work Plan, as requiring additional research and testing. If the organization is complex, with many different services targeting many different customers, the future business model may need to be defined by each service area. If the current business model discussion has revealed inconsistencies in mission compatibility, the Future Business Model Worksheet may reflect attempts to reduce these.

WORKSHEET 5.1 **Future Business Model** (Sample)

This discussion asks you to consider your nonprofit's future situation.

Scope	Includes	Does <u>not</u> include
Geographic service area	Greater metropolitan area, our primary county	We will not serve people in the suburbs outside our city or the surrounding counties
Customers served	+ Adults ages 18–64 + Both men and women + Families of clients (where appropriate) + With selected disorders: • Schizophrenia • Major depression • Forensic • Mental health and substance abuse Will consider: • Age 65+ • Individuals with developmental disabilities	Same as current, except for the two groups we are considering: age 65+ and individuals with developmental disabilities
Programs or services offered	Same, plus will include + Increased postdischarge case management for hospitalized patients + Crisis services + More case management in general	Will continue to exclude - Services for adolescents - Acute inpatient - Skilled nursing facility
Funding sources	Future sources of funding and why we will pursue these sources: + We will seek to increase the level of government funding: the main funding source that covers the type of services we provide and the types of customers we serve + We intend to seek more foundation funding and earned income	Funding sources we will not seek: Other than corporate (mentioned in our Current Business Model worksheet), there is no source that we would intentionally exclude. However, the reality is that we are dependent on government funding

IDENTITY STATEMENT

The identity statement is the aggregate of all the components that have been produced by Tools 1–5. It summarizes these components into a succinct statement that captures the essence of what the nonprofit is.

Use, outcomes, and measures

SITUATION: When is this tool useful?	OUTCOMES: How will you know you've achieved your goals?
An identity statement is useful when there is a need to . . . • Clarify who the nonprofit is; for example, it is very useful as part of an orientation process for new board or staff members • Create a sense of teamwork throughout the organization • Improve external communications; develop a consistent message	Indicators and measures of outcomes: • All board and staff have the same shared understanding of the nonprofit; new board and staff members are quickly integrated into the group • Increased communication and improved morale • Better understanding of the nonprofit among external stakeholders

How should you use it?

The identity statement should be reviewed regularly at staff and board meetings, and the components of it revisited when you sense that your environment may be about to change significantly. The tool contributes to the ongoing development of capacity for strategic thinking and acting.

TOOL 1 2 3 4 5 6 7 8 9 10

WORKSHEET 6.1 Identity Statement (Sample)

Components of identity statement	Your nonprofit's identity statement
We advance our mission of	assisting people with mental illness to achieve optimum recovery and functioning in the community
... and seek to *(impact)*	improve the quality of life and independence of individuals whose mental distress, emotional crisis, or mental illness is interfering with their lives
by serving *(customers)*	seriously mentally ill (SMI) adults (ages 18–64)
in *(geographic area)*	our four-county region
through *(programs or services)*	a range of community-based, recovery-oriented rehabilitation programs
and emphasizing our competitive advantages of	our strong community-oriented approach, well-established reputation, and delivery of recovery-oriented (not medical model) clinical and community-based services that emphasize empowerment over pathologizing our clients.
We are sustainable by *(funding sources)*	having a diversified fund development effort, including emphasis on foundation grants and individual donors, supplementing our earned income from government contracts.

STRATEGY SCREEN

The Strategy Screen is a tool for determining, in advance, the criteria for adopting any new strategy to answer the Big Question facing your organization.

Use, outcomes, and measures

SITUATION: When is this tool useful?	OUTCOMES: How will you know you've achieved your goals?
A Strategy Screen is useful when there is a need to . . . • Determine the values-based criteria that will guide future strategic decisions before the critical moment of decision arrives	Indicators and measures of outcomes: • Greater awareness of what is important to the nonprofit and of how well various options line up with its values • Greater consistency and intentionality in strategic decision making

How should you use it?

The Strategy Screen will help ensure that your strategic choices are conscious. The Strategy Screen captures your view of the important criteria that any new strategic decisions must meet. If you decide to violate one of the criteria, however, you will do so knowingly. For example, perhaps a criterion is that all new programs must break even within one year. Then a new, otherwise attractive opportunity arises that will lose money for three years. It is too important to your mission to pass up. So you consciously violate that criterion.

Before selecting and implementing a new strategy, your nonprofit will need to evaluate the impact of the strategy using specific decision-making criteria, that is, its "Strategy Screen." You should develop the Strategy Screen after you have created your identity statement and before you determine the current Big Question facing your nonprofit (that is, the trend, factor, or event in your marketplace that you have decided to address by forming a strategy). The specific criteria of the Strategy Screen depend on your organization's mission, competitive advantage(s), and situation. The criteria are different for each organization and most likely need to change over time as your nonprofit adapts to changes in the environment.

The strategy must support

- *Your organization's mission (assuming that your mission does not need to change)*

- *Your organization's competitive advantages (specific to the situation, the Big Question facing your nonprofit)*

Include additional criteria, as you see fit, such as requiring that the strategy

- *Meet specified financial criteria (e.g., a new program must pay for itself)*

- *Meet quality criteria (e.g., new services must be of high quality)*

- *Meet criteria related to your organization's geographic and customer scope*

- *Position your organization as a leader*

Your Strategy Screen criteria (*Sample*)

List the criteria your group has selected for its Strategy Screen.

Our strategy must . . .

- Support our mission

- Enhance our competitive advantages, our strong community-oriented approach, well-established reputation, and delivery of recovery-oriented (not medical model) clinical and community-based services that emphasize empowerment over pathologizing our clients

- Be financially viable

- Be consistent with our culture

- Support us in moving to the next stage of our organization's development

BIG QUESTION

The Big Question Tool is designed to move you toward consensus on your understanding of a major opportunity or challenge facing the organization prior to developing a strategy to address it.

Use, outcomes, and measures

SITUATION: When is this tool useful?	OUTCOMES: How will you know you've achieved your goals?
A Big Question is useful when there is a need to . . .	Indicators and measures of outcomes:
• Clarify a great opportunity or challenge facing the nonprofit	• Agreement by all participants on the nature of the Big Question

How should you use it?

If there is any doubt about how to describe a Big Question for the organization, this tool will provide clarification. With agreement on the Big Question, the organization can develop a strategy that responds to that opportunity or challenge.

Use this tool when you are ready to ask yourself what Big Questions face your organization. (See Chapter 6 for a complete description of this concept.) The discussion of business models (current and future) and trends in previous tools is critical to identifying Big Questions. Knowing your nonprofit's position in its market and what makes it different is also important.

Start by having the group brainstorm the Big Question. Remember, these are opportunities, competitive challenges, or business model challenges. After about five to ten minutes, you'll have a good list. Then narrow the list down, finding consensus on the most significant and pressing issue you face, or at least on the one that you want to tackle first. There may be more than one Big Question, but for this exercise, just choose one. Once your group has come to consensus on your Big Question, move on to finalize your identity statement and use your Strategy Screen. The sample below shows how one organization moved from a laundry list of important concerns to a final Big Question.

Some of our most important questions are:

Leadership transition: How do we replace our revered founding CEO who is so intertwined with our identity and success?

Increased competition: How do we address increased competition in our geographic area that is threatening our market position and decreasing our market share?

Reliance on government funding: Given that we are, by design, heavily reliant on government support, how do we protect ourselves against fluctuation in public funding?

Lack of overhead for upgrades: Given our reliance on government funding, which barely covers basic overhead costs, how do we maintain our facilities up to "best practice" standards, ensure that our staff get the clinical training they need to maintain our quality standards, and provide adequate compensation to recruit and retain top-notch clinical experts?

New program opportunity: Should we compete for the new contract that will be available from the county?

Our most important ("big") questions in priority order are:

Leadership transition: How do we replace our revered founding CEO who is so intertwined with our identity and success?

How do we become less heavily reliant on government funding?

The Big Question we will focus on today is:

How do we replace our CEO? What kind of person do we seek? (which gets at the question of how we want to be perceived in the community)

Write your proposed strategy here:

We will not try to find a clone of our current leader, but will view this transition as an opportunity to reinvent the organization to a large extent. We will immediately begin to plan a well-thought-out transition process. We will strengthen the board with new members who are not tied to our CEO, but bring new skills and relationships. We will devote more energy to training our senior management team so that it can provide real leadership in the transition period. We will secure the services of an experienced consultant who understands our situation, is sensitive to our culture, and will be a partner with us in navigating the road ahead to achieve the outcomes we seek. We will develop this strategy further as we go along.

Does the strategy help us answer our Big Question? How?

Our strategy responds to our Big Question by identifying steps to get started on and characteristics of what we want to get out of the transition. It will have to be further developed once we get started thinking about the transition.

Does the strategy meet our Strategy Screen criteria? Is it consistent with our values?

1. Support our mission

2. Enhance our competitive advantage, our strong community-oriented approach, and well-established reputation

3. Be financially viable

4. Be consistent with our culture

5. Support us in moving to the next stage of our organization's development

We have reviewed this strategy against our Strategy Screen and it meets all our criteria. The two-year time frame for achieving our strategy requires that we begin implementation immediately.

Note: If the strategy fails the Strategy Screen, go back and formulate a new strategy. Keep this up until you find a strategy that satisfies your criteria.

NEXT STEPS WORK PLAN

This is a work plan for the activities that need to be accomplished subsequent to a Real-Time Strategic Planning kick-off session. It consists of two components: activities to develop the strategy to address the current Big Question, and activities that the nonprofit will engage in to build its capacity for ongoing strategic thinking and acting.

Use, outcomes, and measures

SITUATION: When is this tool useful?	OUTCOMES: How will you know you've achieved your goals?
A next steps tool is useful when there is a need to . . . • Make sure that everyone knows what needs to be done following the Real-Time Strategic Planning kick-off session • Identify whether the activities being pursued are having their intended outcomes • Develop the nonprofit's capacity for strategic thinking and acting	Indicators and measures of outcomes: • Improved ability of the nonprofit to achieve its desired outcomes by monitoring progress of completed activities • Use of the most appropriate tools to address Big Question • Increased awareness of the nonprofit's situation, its environment, trends, competitors • Increased ability to proactively spot trends and understand how they may impact the nonprofit • More rapid formation of ideas for addressing the nonprofit's situation • Formation of more creative and innovative ideas

How should you use it?

The Next Steps Work Plan Tool is essential to Real-Time Strategic Planning. You can use this tool to realize the full impact of your Real-Time Strategic Planning kick-off session. As with any tool, it is only useful if it is used. It is important that this tool be reviewed periodically. Use the review to track progress, make modifications where needed, and remotivate the group to do the work it needs to do to be strategic. By "living" this tool, and monitoring the outcomes, your organization will reap the benefits of being more strategic.

WORKSHEET 9.1 Next Steps Work Plan (Sample)

Complete the worksheet to show the primary activities that you will need to perform as you move forward to put your strategy to use.

Activity (examples)	Responsible person(s)	Time frame (post-session)	Description of tasks; comments (examples)
Create the Strategy Road Map and review it with the strategy team and then with all staff and board members.	Executive director (ED)	See Tasks	Create draft: 1 week post-session Review with strategy team: 1.5 weeks post-session Distribute to everyone: 2 weeks post-session
Schedule time at staff meetings and board meetings to review the Strategy Road Map, monitor progress, and make adjustments as needed.	ED	Review once a month	Monitor to make sure that time is set aside for this discussion. Identify any adjustments that should be made to the Strategy Road Map.
We will focus on our Big Question and on implementing our strategy. We will develop a work plan for the executive transition.	Board chair (lead); special board committee for executive transition created; ED closely involved	Work plan developed within 1 month of Real-Time Strategic Planning session and spanning the next 2+ years	The work plan will encompass identification of skills, experience, etc., required to take our nonprofit through the next stage, given the current and future environment we face, given the current and future environment we face, recruitment, selection, training, etc. The plan will incorporate a focus on celebrating our achievements to date and the successes that our founding executive director has created, along with the organization as a whole. It will place heavy emphasis on the impact of change on our staff and volunteers, and the community as a whole, and will strive to ensure a smooth transition.

Worksheet 9.1 Next Steps Work Plan (Sample–continued)

Activity (examples)	Responsible person(s)	Time frame (post-session)	Description of tasks; comments (examples)
Select and use 1–2 tools for building strategic thinking and acting capacity; choose tools that fit our nonprofit's needs and culture.	Strategy team	Decide on tools to try: 2 weeks post-session.	Choose one or two tools, such as: • Given the increasing competition in our market, we will focus on tools that will keep us up to date on trends and help us consider their impact on our organization. We will start by setting aside at least 15–20 minutes once a month at staff and board meetings for a discussion of trends and competitors, identifying and tracking any Big Questions that arise, etc. • To maintain our competitive advantage of excellent customer service, we will develop and periodically conduct a short survey of our customers.

Worksheet 9.1 Next Steps Work Plan (Sample–continued)

Activity (examples)	Responsible person(s)	Time frame (post-session)	Description of tasks; comments (examples)
Monitor use of tools. Allow 6 months to use the tool and then assess its usefulness. Depending on assessment, continue to use the tool(s) or choose other tool(s).	Strategy team	Meet once a month to review what we have learned. After 6 months: assess the usefulness of each tool and decide whether to keep using it or try another.	A subset of our Strategy Team, those who have contacts with leaders in our field will seek information regarding programs or services and populations that we are considering serving (per our future business model). They will conduct 1–2 informal interviews each quarter. Strategy Team members who have strong ties to community leaders will check with their informal networks to learn of any community trends that may impact our nonprofit. They will touch base with one colleague every other week; they will nurture their network. When our Strategy Team meets (monthly), we will share what we have learned and consider how it might impact our Strategy Road Map.
Schedule annual Real-Time Strategic Planning renewal session.	ED	As needed	Use this process again.

STRATEGY ROAD MAP

The first part of the Strategy Road Map pulls together all the components developed through the use of the previous tools and provides a concise summary of the process through which participants developed a compelling sense of the nonprofit's identity that resonates with the group. The second part of the Strategy Road Map provides a summary of the process through which participants formed a strategy to address the nonprofit's selected current Big Question. This includes the choice of the Big Question, formation and testing of proposed strategies using the Strategy Screen, and development of a work plan to create and implement the strategy and to enhance the organization's capacity for ongoing strategic thinking and acting.

Use, outcomes, and measures

SITUATION: When is this tool useful?	OUTCOMES: How will you know you've achieved your goals?
A Strategy Road Map is useful when there is a need to . . . • Document the Real-Time Strategic Planning session in a concise way to keep the outcomes front of mind and to share information throughout the nonprofit • Bring new staff and board members up to speed regarding the organization • Provide funders with a document that summarizes the strategy formation work and outcomes	Indicators and measures of outcomes: • Clarity about organizational identity, current issues, and the most significant challenge or opportunity at present and how it is being addressed • Improved and faster understanding of, and orientation to, the organization; more consistent communications • Better understanding of the value of this process for funders; ability to better distinguish it from strategic planning; willingness to support it

TOOL 1 2 3 4 5 6 7 8 9 10

How should you use it?

The Strategy Road Map is a living document. You should review it periodically to reinforce your nonprofit's identity and its need to keep eyes and ears open to events and trends in the environment. The Strategy Road Map can remind you of the importance of addressing your Big Questions and can help to monitor implementation of your strategies that do so. In addition to serving as a work plan for implementing your strategies, it outlines the various activities and practical tools that your group will use to enhance its ability to think and act strategically. Review this work plan at staff and board meetings so you develop a habit of using the tools; identifying opportunities and issues in the environment; considering their implications; developing ideas about sound, innovative ways that your nonprofit can address its Big Questions; and discussing the Big Questions and strategies as a team.

Based on these ongoing discussions, periodically revise the Strategy Road Map as necessary. We recommend at least an annual follow-up session after which the Strategy Road Map should also be updated.

The agenda for the Real-Time Strategic Planning kick-off session essentially forms an outline for the Strategy Road Map. Drawing on your notes from the session, complete each of the sections listed below.

Description of Real-Time Strategic Planning

Goals or reasons why our nonprofit engaged in this process

We wanted to engage in a full strategic planning process, but so many of us had negative experiences with strategic planning, we just couldn't put everyone through it again. We just don't have the time and energy for that. Also, our founding CEO (our leader for the past three decades!) is retiring in 2 years; we need to focus our energy on preparing for this major change. However, we know we have to pay attention to what's going on in our environment; our competition is growing, and there are trends in our field that will impact how we provide care for people with serious mental illness. So, we need a process that's focused, that won't take a lot of time, and will help us address the issues we face right now. The Real-Time Strategic Planning process seems designed to meet our needs.

Our nonprofit's mission statement and identity statement

Attach completed worksheet W6.1.

To help seriously mentally ill adults achieve optimum recovery and function in the community

We advance our mission and seek to improve the quality of life and independence of individuals whose mental distress, emotional crisis, or mental illness is interfering with their lives by serving seriously mentally ill (SMI) adults (ages 18–64) in a four-county region. We do this through a range of community-based, recovery-oriented rehabilitation programs. Our competitive advantages are our strong community-oriented approach, well-established reputation, and delivery of recovery-oriented (not medical model) clinical and community-based services that emphasize empowerment over pathologizing our clients. We have a diversified fund development effort, including emphasis on foundation grants and individual donor which supplements our earned income from government contracts.

Overview of session and introductions

Attendees introduce themselves, explain their role with the organization, and why they work for us or serve on our board. Record on the chart below.

Session date: _____

Session leader: _____

Note taker: _____

Location of session: _____

Name	Staff or board member	Reason for working with nonprofit
Dr. Jane Ellis	Board member	Her sister has SMI and was served by us; Dr. Ellis was very impressed with the quality of care and the kindness and competency of the staff
Susan Barney	Staff	Did her graduate school internship here and loved the work; saw how much the services help the SMI and how well we work with the community

History and background of our nonprofit

We were established in the early 1970s, at the beginning of the government's "de-institutionalization" of the SMI population. We were the first such organization in our region. Our purpose was, and continues to be, to help adults (under age 65) who have SMI to transition to living as independently as possible in the community. We have grown significantly over the years and are a leader in our field, in our region, and in our state. We continually adapt to changes in our field and seek to improve our services and achieve better outcomes for our clients. Our founding CEO led us through this growth and established our leadership position; she is retiring in 2 years.

Impact that our nonprofit is seeking to achieve

- Community acceptance of individuals who have SMI (reduction in stigma); integration of our clients into the community as productive citizens

- Improved quality of life for adults with SMI

- Help the adult SMI population become more independent

Our current business model

Attach completed worksheets W1.1, W2.1, and W2.2.

We serve a four-county area surrounding our clinic.

Our customers are ages 18–64 with a variety of disorders that are generally classified as serious mental illness (SMI).

We offer a range of programs including housing, outreach to homeless, day treatment, respite care, and case management services.

We rely to a significant degree on government funding.

Overview of competition

See completed worksheet W3.1.

Note: We have direct competitors, substitutable competitors, and resource competitors. Our focus here and in our strategy development process is on our direct competitors—those who are most similar to us. We seek to learn from our resource competitors regarding how to attract more media attention (we are already pretty good at this) and how to attract top community and business leaders to our board. We would like to get better at attracting these kinds of resources because, with the upcoming retirement of our longtime CEO, we anticipate that several of our longtime board members will retire as well. We need to get better at attracting young community leaders, as this will be important to our future.

Our market is becoming increasingly competitive. We used to be the only organization providing services for deinstitutionalized adults with SMI, but now there are several, including for-profit corporations that can afford the latest in clinical care and that compete for staff by offering higher salaries.

Summary of our competitors and how our nonprofit compares

What we admire about each of our top direct or substitutable competitors; what we can learn from them and from our resource competitors; how our nonprofit compares and what it does well. See completed worksheet W3.1.

Our competitors are strong and growing. Although we compare well, we cannot rest on our laurels. Our competition has strong clinical skills (for the most part) and is growing, and the population with SMI is growing somewhat. We need to continue to ensure that the quality of care we provide is top-notch and that we attract the best staff possible (one advantage that our competitors seem to have—especially our for-profit competitor—is more resources for clinical care, as well as newer facilities). We also need to consider expanding to other populations, such as those with developmental disabilities (DD) and the senior SMI population (age 65+). The latter population is growing and our current clients are aging, so we need to consider their needs for continuing service from us; we do not want to have them age out of our services and transition to one of our competitors who provides services for adults with SMI who are 65+.

Our nonprofit's competitive advantage

Description of competitive advantage: list the advantages mentioned by the group and identify top competitive advantage (or top three). See Handout 3.1.

We have deep roots in the community that were established over many decades, and a strong understanding of the community's needs; we have an outstanding reputation.

We deliver recovery-oriented (not medical model) clinical and community-based services that emphasize empowerment over pathologizing our clients.

Current and future trends and their impact

Summarize the discussion about trends. Attach completed Worksheet W4.1.

Generally, we compare well, but we need to keep our focus (we cannot be all things to all people) and continue to ensure that the quality of care we provide is top-notch and that we attract the best staff possible. The need for our services is increasing, especially among the age 65+ population that we do not currently serve. Government funding is stable, but is increasingly focused on case management.

Future business model

Attach completed Worksheet W5.1.

We will expand our emphasis on case management services, as this will be a focus of government funding in the future. In addition, we will place more focus on residential community-based care. Because this type of care is less costly than more intense levels of care, the government will put increased emphasis on it. This is a strength that we can build upon. We will keep on top of trends in clinical care, as ongoing improvements lead to improved outcomes and lower costs over time. These improvements are important as we want to provide the best quality to our customers and attract the best, most competent staff. The aging of the population is also something we need to address. We do not want our customers to age out of our programs (which is the case now since we do not serve the SMI population age 65+). We also need to consider serving the developmentally disabled population, as we have the expertise to do this, government funding for this is available, and our competitors do not currently provide many services to this population.

Our Strategy Screen

Attach completed Worksheet W7.1.

Our strategy must . . .

- Support our mission
- Enhance our competitive advantages, our strong community-oriented approach, well-established reputation, and delivery of recovery-oriented (not medical model) clinical and community-based services that emphasize empowerment over patholo-gizing our clients
- Be financially viable
- Be consistent with our culture
- Support us in moving to the next stage of our organization's development

Big Questions facing our nonprofit

List top question(s). Identify your top priority Big Question to be addressed. Attach completed Worksheet W8.1.

Some of our most important questions are:

1. Leadership transition: How do we replace our revered founding CEO who is so intertwined with our identity and success?

2. Increased competition: How do we address the increased competition in our geographic area that is threatening our market position and decreasing our market share?

3. Reliance on government funding: Given that we are, by design, heavily reliant on government funding, how do we protect ourselves against fluctuation in govern-ment funding?

4. Lack of overhead for upgrades: Given our reliance on government funding, which barely covers basic overhead costs, how do we maintain our facilities up to "best practice" standards, ensure that our staff is provided the clinical training they need to maintain our quality standards, and provide adequate compensation to recruit and retain top-notch clinical experts?

Our Big Question

Leadership transition: How do we replace our revered founding CEO who is so inter-twined with our identity and success? And, how do we make sure that the transition is smooth, honoring our past while moving us to the next stage of our organization and preparing us for the future and the challenges it presents?

Our selected strategy to address our Big Question:

Summarize our strategy and demonstrate that it passes our Strategy Screen.

We will not try to find a clone of our current leader, but will view this transition as an opportunity to reinvent the organization to a large extent. We will immediately begin to plan a well-thought-out transition process. We will secure the services of an experienced consultant who understands our situation, is sensitive to our culture, and will be a partner with us in navigating the road ahead to achieve the outcomes we seek. We will develop this strategy further as we go along. We will strengthen the board with new members who are not tied to our CEO, and who bring new skills and relationships. We will devote more energy to training our senior management team so that it can provide real leadership in the transition period. We have reviewed this strategy against our Strategy Screen and it meets all our criteria. The 2-year time frame for achieving our strategy requires that we begin implementation immediately.

Next steps

Outline our next steps, including developing, implementing, and monitoring our strategy and its impact on our Big Question, and complete our work plan for developing capacity for strategic thinking and acting. Attach completed Worksheet W9.1.

Our work plan for the next steps in creating and implementing our strategy is outlined on the next pages. We will monitor our progress to ensure our desired outcomes and make adjustments as needed.

Work Plan (Sample)

Activity	Responsible person(s)	Time frame (post-session)	Description of tasks; comments
Create the Strategy Road Map and review it with the strategy team and then with all staff and board members	Executive director	See Tasks	Create draft: 1 week post-session Review with strategy team: 1.5 weeks post-session Distribute to everyone: 2 weeks post-session
Schedule time at staff meetings and board meetings to review the Strategy Road Map and monitor progress, make adjustments as needed	Executive director	Review once a month	Monitor to make sure that time is set aside for this discussion. Identify any adjustments that should be made to the Strategy Road Map.
We will focus on our Big Question and implementing our strategy. We will develop a work plan for the executive transition.	Board chair (lead); special board committee for executive transition created; executive director closely involved	Work plan developed within 1 month of Real-Time Strategic Planning session and spanning the next 2+ years	The work plan will encompass identification of skills, experience, etc., required to take us to the next stage, given the current and future environment we face; recruitment; selection; training; etc. It will incorporate a focus on celebrating our achievements to date and the successes that our founding executive director created, along with the organization as a whole. It will place heavy emphasis on the impact of change on our staff and volunteers and the community as a whole, and will strive to ensure a smooth transition.

Worksheet 10.1 Strategy Road Map (Sample–continued)

Activity	Responsible person(s)	Time frame (post-session)	Description of tasks; comments
Select and use 1–2 tools for building strategic-thinking and -acting capacity; choose tools that fit our nonprofit's needs and culture.	Strategy team	Decide on tools to try: 2 weeks post-session. Meet once a month to review what we have learned. After 6 months assess the usefulness of each tool and decide whether to keep using it or try another.	Choose one or two tools, such as: • Given the increasing competition on our market, we will focus on tools that will keep us up to date on trends and help us consider their impact on our organization. We will start by setting aside at least 15–20 minutes once a month at staff meetings and at board meetings for a discussion of trends and competitors, identifying and tracking any Big Questions that arise, etc. • To maintain our competitive advantage of excellent customer service, we will periodically conduct a short survey of our customers.
Monitor use of tools. Allow a 6-month period to use the tool and then assess its usefulness. Depending on our assessment, continue to use the tool(s) or choose other tool(s).			A subset of our Strategy Team, those who have contacts with leaders in our field, will seek information regarding programs or services and populations that we are considering serving (per our future business model). They will conduct 1–2 informal interviews each quarter. Strategy Team members who have strong ties to community leaders will check with their informal networks to learn of any community trends that may impact our nonprofit. They will touch base with one colleague every other week; they will nurture their network. When our Strategy Team meets, we will share what we have learned and consider how it might impact our Strategy Road Map.
Schedule annual Real-Time Strategic Planning session.	Executive director	As needed	Use this process again.

References

The works listed below were directly consulted, and in some cases the authors were interviewed, in the initial phase of this initiative.

Aaker, David A. 1996. *Building Strong Brands.* New York: The Free Press.

Allison, Mike, and Jude Kaye. 2005. *Strategic Planning for Nonprofit Organizations,* 2nd ed. San Francisco: Jossey-Bass.

Angelica, Emil. 2001. *The Fieldstone Alliance Nonprofit Guide to Crafting Effective Mission & Vision Statements.* Saint Paul, MN: Fieldstone Alliance.

Barry, Bryan. 1987. *Strategic Planning Workbook for Nonprofit Organizations.* Saint Paul, MN: Amherst Wilder Foundation. Revised edition, 2003. Saint Paul, MN: Fieldstone Alliance.

Beene, Melanie. 1988. *Autopsy of an Orchestra: An Analysis of Factors Contributing to the Bankruptcy of the Oakland Symphony Orchestra Association.* San Francisco: Melanie Beene & Associates.

Block, Peter. 1981. *Flawless Consulting.* San Francisco: Jossey-Bass.

Brest, Paul. 2003. "What the Nonprofit Sector Can Learn from Home Improvements." *The Nonprofit Quarterly,* 10, no. 4 (Winter).

Bryson, John. 1995. *Strategic Planning for Public and Nonprofit Organizations: A Guide to Strengthening and Sustaining Organizational Achievement.* San Francisco: Jossey-Bass.

Butler, Lawrence M. 2007. *The Nonprofit Dashboard: A Tool for Tracking Progress.* Washington, DC: BoardSource.

Csikszentmihalyi, Mihaly. 1996. *Creativity.* New York: HarperCollins.

Collins, Jim. 2001. *Good to Great: Why Some Companies Make the Leap... and Others Don't*. New York: HarperBusiness.

Collins, Jim and Jerry Porras. 1994. *Built to Last: Successful Habits of Visionary Companies*. New York: HarperBusiness.

Coyne, Kevin P. 1986. "The Anatomy of Sustainable Competitive Advantage." *McKinsey Quarterly* 2 (Spring): 50–65.

Culick, Liza, Kristen Godard, and Natasha Terk. 2004. *The Due Diligence Tool*. Washington, DC: Grantmakers for Effective Organizations.

Eisenberg, Pablo. 2007. "Gates: Role Model in Need of Remodeling." *Chronicle of Philanthropy* 19, no. 10 (March 8): 39–41.

Feldman, Mark L., and Michael F. Spratt. 1999. *Five Frogs on a Log: A CEO's Field Guide to Accelerating the Transition in Mergers, Acquisitions and Gut Wrenching Change*. New York: HarperCollins.

Gladwell, Malcolm. 2005. *Blink: The Power of Thinking without Thinking*. New York: Little, Brown and Company.

Hague, Paul, Nick Hague, and Carol-Ann Morgan. 2004. *Market Research in Practice*. Sterling, VA: Kogan Page, Ltd.

Heft, Lisa. 2002. "Opening Space for Collaboration and Communication with Open Space Technology." *The Facilitator* (Spring): 1–3. <http://www.thefacilitator.com/htdocs/Open%20Space.pdf>. Accessed 16 November 2007.

Hughes, Sandra R. 1999. *To Go Forward, Retreat: The Board Retreat Handbook*. BoardSource. <http://www.boardsource.org/dl.asp?document_id=520>. Accessed 16 November 2007.

Kaplan, Robert, and David P. Norton. 2001. *The Strategy Focused Organization: How Balanced Scorecard Companies Thrive in the New Business Environment*. Boston: Harvard Business School Press.

Kearns, Kevin. 2000. *Private Sector Strategies for Social Sector Success*. San Francisco: Jossey-Bass.

Kelly, Tom. 2005. *The Art of Innovation: Lessons in Creativity from IDEO, America's Leading Design Firm*. New York: Doubleday.

Kaner, Sam. [1996] 2002. *The Facilitator's Guide to Participatory Decision-Making*. Gabriola Island, BC: New Society Publishers.

La Piana, David, with Michaela Hayes. 2005. *Play to Win: The Nonprofit Guide to Competitive Strategy*. San Francisco: Jossey-Bass.

La Piana, David, Liza Culick, Kristen Godard, and William Coy. 2003. *Tool for Assessing Start-Up Organizations*. Washington, DC: Grantmakers for Effective Organizations.

Logic Model Development Guide. January 2004. Battle Creek, MI: W.K. Kellogg Foundation. <http://www.wkkf.org/Pubs/Tools/Evaluation/Pub3669.pdf>. Accessed 7 December 2007.

Lukas, Carol, and Linda Hoskins. 2003. *Fieldstone Alliance Nonprofit Guide to Conducting Community Forums: Engaging Citizens, Mobilizing Communities*. Saint Paul, MN: Fieldstone Alliance.

Manktelow, James. 2004. *Mind Tools: Essential Skills for an Excellent Career*. West Sussex, UK: Mind Tools Ltd.

McFarland, Keith. "A Better Scheme for Strategic Planning." BusinessWeek.com. 19 January 2005. <http://www.businessweek.com/smallbiz/content/jan2005/sb20050119_9832_sb037.htm>. Accessed 19 November 2007.

McLaughlin, Thomas. 2006. *Nonprofit Strategic Positioning*. Hoboken, NJ: John Wiley & Sons.

Mintzberg, Henry. 1994. *The Rise and Fall of Strategic Planning*. New York: The Free Press.

Mintzberg, Henry, Bruce Ahlstand, and Joseph Lampel. 1998. *Strategy Safari*. New York: The Free Press.

Napier, Rod, Clint Sidle, and Patrick Sanaghan. 1996. *High Impact Tools and Activities for Strategic Planning: Creative Techniques for Facilitating Your Organization's Planning Process*. New York: McGraw-Hill.

Neely, Andy, ed. 2002. *Business Performance Measurement*. Cambridge: Cambridge University Press.

Open Space World <www.openspaceworld.org>. Accessed 16 November 2007.

Owen, Harrison. 1997. *Expanding Our Now: The Story of Open Space Technology.* San Francisco: Berrett-Koehler.

———.1997. *Open Space Technology: A User's Guide.* San Francisco: Berrett-Koehler.

Peters, Jeanne and Timothy Wolfred, with Mike Allison, Christina Chan, Jan Masaoka, and Genevieve Llamas. 2001. *Daring to Lead: Nonprofit Executive Directors and Their Work Experience.* San Francisco: CompassPoint.

Porter, M.E. 1996. "What Is Strategy?" *Harvard Business Review* (November-December): 61–78.

———. 1985. *Competitive Advantage: Creating and Sustaining Superior Performance.* New York: The Free Press.

Radtke, Janel M. 1998. *Strategic Communications for Nonprofit Organizations: Seven Steps to Creating a Successful Plan.* New York: John Wiley & Sons.

Ramanujam, Vasudevan, N. Venkatraman, and John C. Camillus. 1986. "Multi-objective Assessment of Effectiveness of Strategic Planning: A Discriminant Analysis Approach." *Academy of Management Journal* 29, no. 2 (June): 347–72.

Rich, Jason R. 2003. *Brain Storm.* Franklin Lakes, NJ: The Career Press.

Schwartz, Peter. 1996. *The Art of the Long View: Planning for the Future in an Uncertain World.* New York: Currency/Doubleday.

Scearce, Diana, and Katherine Fulton. 2004. *What If? The Art of Scenario Thinking for Nonprofits.* San Francisco: Global Business Network.

Simon, Judith Sharken. 1999. *The Fieldstone Alliance Guide to Conducting Successful Focus Groups.* Saint Paul, MN: Fieldstone Alliance.

Stern, Gary J. 1997. *Marketing Workbook for Nonprofit Organizations. Volume II: Mobilize People for Marketing Success.* Saint Paul, MN: Fieldstone Alliance.

Stern, Gary J., and Elana Centor. [1990] 2001. *Marketing Workbook for Nonprofit Organizations. Volume I: Develop the Plan.* 2nd ed. Saint Paul, MN: Fieldstone Alliance.

Weick, Karl E. 1995. *Sensemaking in Organizations*. Thousand Oaks, CA: Sage Publications.

Wolfred, Timothy, with Mike Allison and Jan Masaoka. 1999. *Leadership Lost: A Study on Executive Director Tenure and Experience*. San Francisco: CompassPoint.

Index

d = diagram, *g* = graph, *w* = worksheet, *ws* = work sheet sample,
FG = Facilitator's Guide on CD, **T** = Tools on CD

d = diagram, *g* = graph, *w* = worksheet, *ws* = work sheet sample, **FG** = Facilitator's Guide on CD, **T** = Tools on CD

d = diagram, *g* = graph, *w* = worksheet, *ws* = work sheet sample,
FG = Facilitator's Guide on CD, **T** = Tools on CD

d = diagram, *g* = graph, *w* = worksheet, *ws* = work sheet sample,
FG = Facilitator's Guide on CD, **T** = Tools on CD

d = diagram, *g* = graph, *w* = worksheet, *ws* = work sheet sample,
FG = Facilitator's Guide on CD, **T** = Tools on CD

More results-oriented books from Fieldstone Alliance

Strategic Planning Workbook for Nonprofit Organizations

This classic workbook gives you guidance through five planning steps. Interactive worksheets help you develop the plan, involve others in the process, and measure results. Four planning methods show how to tailor the process to fit your organization's individual needs.

by Bryan Barry   Item #069075   128 pages plus CD

Fieldstone Alliance Nonprofit Guide to
Crafting Effective Mission and Vision Statements

Too often, if you ask four people in a nonprofit what their organization's mission is, you'll get four different answers. This book will help your organization craft a mission statement, vision statement, or both.

by Emil Angelica   Item #06927X   88 pages

Fieldstone Alliance Nonprofit Guide to
Conducting Community Forums

Step-by-step instructions to plan and carry out exciting, successful community forums that will educate the public, build consensus, focus action, or influence policy.

by Carol Lukas and Linda Hoskins   Item #069318   128 pages

Strengthening Nonprofit Performance
A Funder's Guide to Capacity Building

A collection of strategies, steps, and examples that funders can use to get started on or improve their funding to strengthen nonprofit organizations.

by Paul Connolly and Carol Lukas   Item #069377   184 pages

Visit **www.FieldstoneAlliance.org** to learn more about these and many other books on community building, nonprofit management, funder capacity, and violence prevention. You can also sign up to receive our free "Tools You Can Use" e-newsletter. Or call **1-800-274-6024** for a current catalog.

CD-ROM Instructions*

The enclosed CD contains the following items:

- Facilitator's Guide to Real-Time Strategic Planning. (A complete session packet for conducting a strategy formation process within your organization. You may print copies of this material for organization members.)

- Tools 1–27. (Electronic versions of the tools make it easy to fill out worksheets and print handouts.)

- A Nonprofit Strategy Revolutionary Certificate. (Should you want one!)

This material can also be downloaded from the publisher's web site at the URL below. Simply enter this URL in your web browser and use the following code to download the tools.

http://www.FieldstoneAlliance.org/worksheets

Code: W657Nsr08

This material is provided as PDF files. **To view and use the PDF version of the worksheets, you will need to have the latest version of Adobe Reader installed on your computer.** This free software can be downloaded by visiting www.adobe.com.

Also on the disk is a folder with the Facilitator's Guide in rich text format (rtf). This version can be opened in most word processing programs and can be reformatted to meet the needs of your organization's Real-Time Strategic Planning kick-off session.

PLEASE NOTE: You must copy the files from the CD on to your desktop in order to save the material you type in PDF forms. You will not be able to save information back on to the CD.

*NOTE: The CD-ROM has been replaced with the link above to download the files online; all materials from the CD-ROM can be accessed using the URL and code.